GIS
Landscape
Architects

Karen C. Hanna

ESRI Press

ESRI Press, 380 New York Street, Redlands, California 92373-8100

Copyright © 1999 ESRI

All rights reserved. First edition 1999
10 09 08 07 06 05   3 4 5 6 7 8 9 10

Printed in the United States of America

ISBN 1-879102-64-1

Ask for ESRI Press titles at your local bookstore or order by calling 1-800-447-9778. You can also shop online at www.esri.com/esripress. Outside the United States, contact your local ESRI distributor.

ESRI Press titles are distributed to the trade by the following:

In North America, South America, Asia, and Australia:
Independent Publishers Group (IPG)
Telephone (United States): 1-800-888-4741
Telephone (international): 312-337-0747
E-mail: frontdesk@ipgbook.com

In the United Kingdom, Europe, and the Middle East:
Transatlantic Publishers Group Ltd.
Telephone: 44 20 8849 8013
Fax: 44 20 8849 5556
E-mail: transatlantic.publishers@regusnet.com

Contents

Preface

Landscape architects, unsurprisingly, were among the earliest users of geographic information systems, or GIS. A technology that allows designers to model the world in computer databases is singularly well suited to integrate all of the disciplines that affect the landscape architect—urban planning, environmental protection, architecture, civil engineering.

The book you're holding contains ten case studies that depict interesting and important examples of geographic information technology at work. As you read these stories, you'll gain a sense of how the firms involved have thoughtfully applied GIS to their projects and added a powerful tool to their traditional methods.

There's no need to feel overwhelmed by GIS. It's a technology, a tool, a method for approaching your work. The basic principles of landscape architecture remain the same. You'll still follow a design process, although these new tools may modify that process somewhat. Your solutions won't be significantly different, but since the opportunity to test several alternatives is greater, the solutions will probably also be better.

Because your ability to quantify your proposals is much greater with GIS, your client satisfaction will probably also increase. It's often the small intangibles that make the difference in performance and professional reputation. Landscape architects carefully evaluate every aspect of their practices: they hire the best staff they can, they pursue the clients and projects that will satisfy their professional aspirations. They also use the best tools for accomplishing their goals. One tool landscape architects should be using is GIS.

Since I was trained as a landscape architect, I have a strong attachment to the field and I hope that more of the people I still think of as colleagues will discover for themselves the benefits GIS can bring to their profession.

At the same time, I am discovering that the users of GIS need landscape architects who can provide professional input regarding the design process. I like to think of landscape architects as "geographic designers," people who approach spatial problem solving holistically.

Jack Dangermond
President, ESRI

Acknowledgments

A handful of talented people have made it possible, in a very short period of time, to bring this book to print. At ESRI, Bill Miller put the project into motion and provided stimuli at critical points. Christian Harder, head of ESRI Press, orchestrated the production of the manuscript. Many thanks to Pat Breslin for writing the Salton Sea case-study portion of the ModelBuilder™ chapter. Tim Ormsby, Kim Avery, and Ken Meyer provided technical assistance. Michael Hyatt designed the book and did the production, copyediting, and proofreading. Lisa Godin served as project editor and assisted with page layout. As always, Jack Dangermond provided the inspiration and made the full resources of ESRI available to us.

In Fayetteville, I am grateful to my colleagues for their support, especially Dan Bennett and Judy Stone. At the Center for Advanced Spatial Technologies, I am grateful to James Sullens and Big John Wilson for their help.

ESRI would like to thank the team members at the Center for Environmental Management at the University of Redlands—Tim Krantz, Mark Sorensen, Eric Wittner, Waleed Soliman, and Akiyuki Kawasaki—for their help with the GIS modeling tools chapter.

Introduction

GEOGRAPHIC INFORMATION SYSTEMS, or GIS, are fast becoming the pencils and T-squares of this era. They are only tools, but such revolutionary tools that GIS can change the way landscape architects produce plans, read the landscape, integrate public policy, conduct research, and cooperate with other professionals.

In the following chapters, you will see how both large and small firms have put GIS to work for them in traditional and creative ways. From the firm in New York that uses the viewshed-generating capabilities of GIS to help protect an important visual landscape, to the one in Colorado that uses GIS to show communities how the priorities they set can result in very different proposals, to another in Philadelphia that makes calculation of recreation supply and demand a simple task, many landscape architects are realizing that GIS technology is becoming the standard for agencies and design professionals alike.

Why has GIS become so dominant now? The design professions first used geographic information systems thirty years ago. At that time, landscape architects were in the forefront of the technology. In the interim, the design professions have faced many changes. The environmental legislation begun in the 1970s has permeated all levels of government, from federal to local, and greatly affects the private sector as well. With this awakening of an environmental conscience, and with fiscal changes, accountability has become the slogan under which we all operate. It is not enough to prepare wonderfully creative designs, or comprehensive plans that incorporate many points of view; we must provide quantifiable proof that our designs will yield ecological, economic, functional, and scenic benefits. Further, our world seems to function at an ever more frantic pace and this, too, is felt in our design studios. Our clients want perfect plans, lots of alternatives, and all of it in record time. GIS allows us to provide these services without legions of highly trained staff. We do need highly trained people, but a few can now do the work of many.

Concurrently, our public agencies have faced dramatic changes in the way they do business. If accountability is our slogan, it has become their mandate. An informed citizenry puts great pressure on its service sector to provide police protection, social services, land development controls, tax collection, pollution monitoring, trash removal, roadway maintenance, disaster relief, and a host of other activities, with maximum efficiency. Automation has become the key to survival for many of these service providers. The triumvirate of CAD (computer-aided design), AM/FM (automated mapping, facilities management), and GIS has streamlined these operations. Interactive digital technologies overcome distance, and the Internet has become the research library of the late twentieth century.

Owing to their dependence on digital technology, the agencies are moving all their data into digital formats. High-quality paper maps are much less available than they once were, and digital formats abound. Often, private-sector service providers have no choice but to follow the agencies into the digital realm. And, it is no longer sufficient to print digital files and work manually; the clients want their products in digital format, often including the databases and models used to create the solutions.

In addition to introducing digital efficiencies, GIS also offers the advantage of speed. Master plans, comprehensive plans, and management plans once were revised every ten to twenty years. Now these plans are revised at five-year intervals or even more frequently. Because our demographics, economies, and policies change more quickly, our proposals for development and management have to be more flexible. Assumptions on which those plans were based are quickly outdated. Modifications to the plan can now be based on current data rather than some estimate of future conditions. Because so many sectors of our society maintain databases, from real estate brokers to public works departments, current data can be imported into the GIS and used to revise plans and strategies. The master plan becomes a living, changing document, responding to cultural and natural occurrences, not a static image of what might happen.

How has the GIS revolution affected the traditional landscape architecture office? For some, it has changed not at all. Firms that provide their services almost exclusively to private clients, and those that work only on small- to medium-sized sites, may have no need of GIS now, or for the immediate future. Topographical maps are still available in paper form, as are utilities

and soils maps. Aerial photos provide vegetation and land-use data, and there is still no substitute for the site visit. However, those firms that provide services to public clients, and even to some private developers, are finding that GIS is required more and more frequently. As digital data warehouses become more widespread, and as their transfer technologies are improved, many data types will only be maintained in digital format. Already, all the data provided by the U.S. Geological Survey (USGS) is being maintained in digital form. It is still possible to purchase paper maps, but the trend is toward digital files.

For those offices that have adopted GIS as a tool, there are several staffing models. In the simplest of terms, what are needed are design skills and computer skills. Providing the computer skills are several types of personnel: some may be in-house staff and some may be outside consultants.

Landscape architects, with or without significant training, can do the actual GIS work. As with many skills, there are levels of proficiency, but two or three days of training can be enough to get started. Among the ESRI® products, ArcView® GIS software is quite easy to learn. Since it was designed under the direction of Jack Dangermond, who trained as a landscape architect, it is especially user friendly to landscape architects. ArcView GIS, and several of its extensions, allow one to display and print maps and charts, extract data types from complex data sets, combine data types in simple and sophisticated ways, calculate percentages of slope, derive contours, calculate viewsheds, generate statistics, and print reports.

As ArcView GIS continues to be improved, much of the data functionality previously available only with ArcInfo® software is being incorporated into ArcView GIS, with straightforward dialog boxes to guide us. The user support staff at ESRI is also available to answer questions and walk users through the various functions of ArcView GIS and ArcInfo. The new ArcView GIS extension, ModelBuilder, is a set of wizards that takes us step-by-step through some quite sophisticated models, including importation of CADD (computer-aided design and drafting) files. Time really is on our side; these products keep getting better and easier to use.

How are landscape architects using GIS? This is the subject of this book; ten case studies discuss the reasons for using GIS as well as the methods. Two additional chapters address models: the sequence of steps used to achieve results. Chapter eleven covers the GIS Graphic Method, which I developed. The grid version of this method was introduced in *GIS in Site Design*, written by Karen C. Hanna and R. Brian Culpepper, and published by John Wiley & Sons in 1998. The ArcView GIS version of this method is covered in this book in the chapter entitled "Who needs another method?" The last chapter, written by Pat Breslin of ESRI, covers the new ModelBuilder extension, to be released by ESRI in 1999. This is a godsend for GIS novices. Wizards guide you through commonly used models and frequently performed tasks.

The chart below identifies the ways that landscape architects are using GIS at the end of the twentieth century. GIS is used for site design, recreation master planning, visual analysis, comprehensive planning, resource management, and public advocacy. GIS is not just for scientists and engineers; it serves the needs of designers quite well.

How do landscape architects use GIS?

Chapter	Case-study project	Location	Site design	Recreation master planning	Visual analysis	Comprehensive planning	Resource management	Public advocacy
1	Route 66 Streetscape	Albuquerque, New Mexico	×			×		×
2	Olana Viewshed Study	Chatham, New York				×		×
3	Recreation and Development Atlas	Commerce City, Colorado		×	×		×	
4	Tae-Ah Resort Design	South Korea		×	×			
5	Gregory Canyon Visual Analysis	Pala, California		×			×	
6	Recreation and Management Plan	Pikes Peak, Colorado		×		×	×	×
7	Comprehensive Plan	Athens–Clark County, Georgia				×	×	×
8	Restoration Plan	Kissimmee River, Florida		×			×	×
9	Watershed Management	San Francisco, California		×			×	×
10	Recreation Master Plan	Chattanooga, Tennessee		×		×	×	
11	GIS Graphic Method		×	×	×	×		
12	ESRI ModelBuilder		×	×	×	×	×	×

Chapter 1

Formerly glamorous

DURING THE DECADE OF THE FIFTIES, the allure of the open road added mystique to America's love affair with the automobile. At that time the most intriguing of all roads was Route 66, portrayed on television and in movie theaters as the portal to adventure and romance. Over the years, Route 66 has been subsumed by interstate highways, chopped into fragments going nowhere, and annihilated by shopping malls. Little of the original road remains and that little has often been neglected along with the once-busy commercial districts of the towns it connected.

In central Albuquerque, a 17-mile stretch of Route 66 (known as Central Avenue as it passes through town) is still intact, and the city has decided to resurrect those pilgrimages to the past. Albuquerque planners knew that physical improvements such as storefront remodeling and streetscape enhancements would not by themselves return the street to its former glory. They knew that economic incentives and the support of the commercial and residential neighborhoods were also necessary to revitalize Central Avenue.

Documenting the street and its business

The firm of Sites Southwest LLC (Sites SW), landscape architects, planners, and market analysts, was hired to lead a design team to develop economic programs as well as a comprehensive streetscape design for the first 8-mile segment. Sites SW asked for input from the community, made large economic databases available to its in-house planners, and produced illustrative maps and three-dimensional views. The firm used ArcView GIS and databases supplied by the City of Albuquerque or developed by the design team. Aerial photography and other data were moved into GIS formats by Bohannan Huston, Inc., the subconsultant to Sites SW providing photogrammetry and engineering. Already an ArcInfo user, the City of Albuquerque will receive all products of the Central Avenue streetscape/Route 66 project in digital format for inclusion in its citywide GIS.

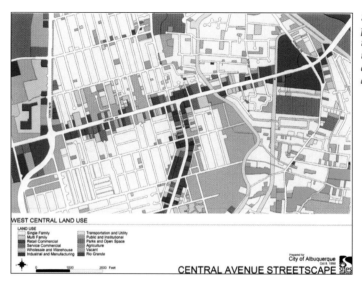

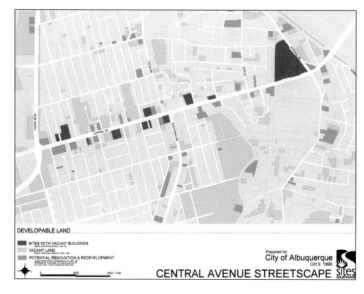

Sites Southwest LLC prepared maps based on information gathered through interviews, county and city records, and field surveys.

Historic character

The City of Albuquerque provided some of the ArcInfo coverages of physical and political data for the study area. The records of assessed parcel values were provided by Bernalillo County. Using aerial photos or other documents, Sites SW developed some of the GIS data maps themselves. The GIS data included street features such as centerlines, islands, curbs, curb-cuts, utilities, traffic signals, rights-of-way, intersections, parcel boundaries, building footprints, flood hazard areas, zoning, land use, assessed values, and ownership. Because these themes were fully developed as GIS layers, they include extensive tables linked to each map. The tables allow sophisticated questions to be posed and answers or reports to be generated, which planners and landscape architects can then use in making design decisions and in defending those decisions. If, for example, the traffic department wants to know how many curb-cuts are eliminated by each design proposal, the GIS can give that answer effortlessly.

These existing databases were expanded with additional information from city planning staff and local businesspeople. Staff and neighborhood representatives took Sites SW on walking and driving tours of their neighborhoods, providing information about vacant lots and rating the conditions of buildings. The project team then made an evaluation of the current improvement value for each property and balanced that against the existing land value. This rating exercise helped the design team identify properties with redevelopment potential. When coupled with the condition assessment, this information helped the team decide between renovating existing buildings and demolishing them. Priority was given to saving existing buildings, especially those with historic character.

In addition to evaluating the properties, the team assessed the economic health of the street. Business owners in each of five sectors were interviewed so the team could gain an understanding of their success and how the businesspeople thought they could improve. The purpose of these economic evaluations was to select the best economic incentives to offer within each sector. Since all sectors do not serve the same type of customers, they do not have the same needs. Low-interest business loans, seed funds for capital improvements, public land acquisitions, and public redevelopment projects are examples of economic programs that will be used to stimulate the business environment on Central Avenue. Related programs include tourism promotion, increased police protection, crime prevention through environmental design, and new community facilities.

Cadastral data maps of features such as right-of-way widths and parcel boundaries were augmented with qualitative assessment maps depicting, for instance, redevelopment potential.

The voice of the people

Four types of meetings brought the neighborhoods into the design process: an initial public meeting, preference surveys, a "visioning" workshop, and two design charettes. The design team introduced the project at the initial meeting, where they described its scope, method, and anticipated outcomes and listened to the community's expectations.

The preference surveys were used to identify desirable characteristics of street furnishings and transportation features. During the preference surveys, several photographs of features, such as benches or crosswalks, were displayed. By design, the photos were not taken in the local area so that participants' feelings about the neighborhood would not interfere with their judgment about the features themselves. Participants then selected their favorite version of a bench or a crosswalk or other streetscape feature. These preference surveys defined the designer's palette and helped build support in the communities along Central Avenue.

The visioning workshop included several meetings to develop the major goals of the economic incentives and the streetscape design phase of the project. These meetings brought ideas into focus for business owners, neighborhood representatives, utility company representatives, city planners, social services agencies, and city public works personnel.

Two design charettes were held in each neighborhood. Residents, business owners, city planning staff, public works staff, family and community services personnel, and utilities representatives all responded directly to the design proposals for Central Avenue. As suggestions were made for proposed features, such as pavement, street furnishings, and plantings, each participant was able to express his or her opinion about the suitability of that component. While "design by committee" is not always successful, the landscape architects were the final arbiters of aesthetics, function, safety, and sustainability.

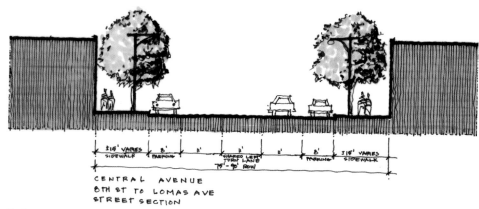

Preference surveys help designers identify the desirable qualities of proposed features.

A long, narrow site analysis

Any corridor 8.3 miles long will have a certain amount of variation, both along its length and in the connections to its adjacent neighborhoods. Sites SW identified five distinct sectors of Central Avenue. The rights-of-way vary from 75 feet in width in the older, eastern end of the study area to 125 feet at the west end. The types of businesses and land uses vary as well.

Near downtown Albuquerque, at the eastern end of the project, there are many offices and service businesses, and a few retail stores. Moving westward, the street caters to tourists who come to visit the nearby Old Town, zoo, aquarium, botanical garden, and scenic Rio Grande Bosque. This is the most dynamic sector of the corridor and the city would like to see this economic vitality extended westward, across the Rio Grande to the Atrisco district.

The Atrisco area includes older businesses, some in decline. It also includes the only two large discount retail outlets on Central Avenue. Moving westward, the next district flanks Old Coors Road. A number of residences are mixed in with the retail stores in this portion of the street.

The western end of the Central Avenue corridor, at Coors Boulevard, is the newest, and one of the most rapidly expanding residential sections of Albuquerque. Businesses here serve the adjoining neighborhoods and private investment is strong. The city wants to maintain high standards in new development here.

Economic maps generated by the GIS were used to delineate these district boundaries. New database tables showed the economic indicators and redevelopment potential for each parcel. This information was combined with notes from site visits, photographs of building facades, and the GIS theme of existing land use to find the nodes of business activity. The newly created GIS themes of "renovation potential" and "business health," described above, helped in defining the edges, as well as the character of each district. This digital site analysis provided the structure for streetscape designs that developed during the neighborhood design charettes.

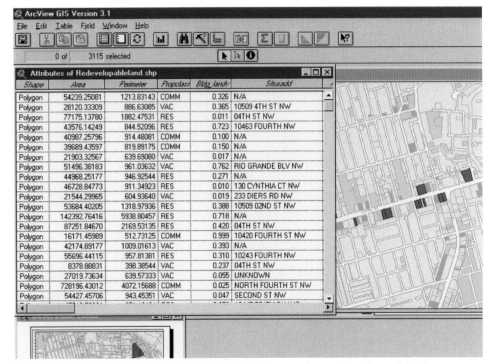

GIS can create economic indicator maps directly from tables or with input from city staff, local businesspeople, or residents.

Streetscape concepts

The two districts east of the Rio Grande have tourist potential and will emphasize the historic characters of Old Town Albuquerque and Route 66. The Atrisco district will also feature its assortment of historic buildings. The two districts at the west end of the project will be identified with the character of the neighborhoods they serve. The goal at this end of the corridor is to set quality design standards to maintain long-term property values and reinforce the economic viability of the area. Some properties at the west end of the project have also been identified for residential infill.

The Central Avenue streetscape/ Route 66 project also makes proposals for streetscape improvements within the right-of-way. Concurrently, the city is establishing a design review process to set standards for redevelopment beyond the front property lines.

Even when the reviewing body includes only professional designers, 3-D views expedite an understanding of the proposals. The 3-D capabilities have long been one of its selling points, and 3-D views are increasingly easy to generate.

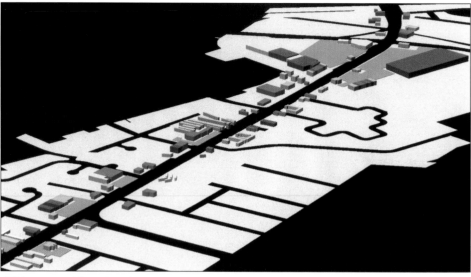

GIS is renowned for making "pretty maps." Recent advances make it much easier to generate three-dimensional views. 3-D views are much more readily understood by citizens and staff alike, and help the designers in visualizing spatial proportions.

To GIS or not to GIS?

There were several compelling reasons to use GIS on this project. The City of Albuquerque is already using GIS throughout its operations. Redevelopment proposals can be entered in the database to see how new productive businesses could increase the overall tax revenue for the district. When this project has been implemented, the "record drawings," in CAD format, will be used to update the GIS files for the street. Both CAD and GIS can be used for estimating installation and maintenance costs.

The GIS allowed the evaluations made by the staff and outside experts to be quickly turned into maps and tables of the project area. The maps were used to determine the boundaries of each subdistrict so that meaningful variations in the design concepts along the corridor could be developed. The tables were used to produce cost estimates for each alternative. This is a perfect example of planning and landscape architecture working together to make robust proposals—not just economic programs and not just physical design, but a synthesis of the two.

Acknowledgments

Thanks to George Radnovich of Sites Southwest, Albuquerque, New Mexico.

Chapter 2

Hudson River artist

THOSE WHO HAVE VISITED the Smithsonian Institution may have seen some of the more than two thousand oils and sketches by Frederick E. Church in the museum's collection. The inspiration for many of Church's landscapes was the view from his home at Olana, in the Hudson River Valley. Though he painted such remote places as the great American West and the Andes of South America, he returned again and again to paint the low hills and majestic sweep of the Hudson River. The State of New York now owns Olana and operates it as a historic park.

In an effort to protect this famous view, the Columbia Land Conservancy (CLC) sought the services of The Saratoga Associates, landscape architects, in Saratoga Springs, New York. Historical material and natural inventories were provided by the Department of Environmental Conservation and the Office of Parks, Recreation, and Historic Preservation, both agencies of the State of New York. The Saratoga Associates engaged Crawford and Associates of Hudson, New York, to prepare the digital basemaps for their work.

The Saratoga Associates' mission was to study the viewshed from Olana and find those sites where new buildings would be hidden from view. Thirty-five feet is the height of most new, residential structures in the area, so 35 feet was used as the test height for possible intrusions in the view.

Frederick Church was known for his panoramic paintings of scenes such as the Hudson River Valley.

Viewsheds

A viewshed is the area that is visible from a given point. The GIS calculates a viewshed using a digital elevation model (DEM). A DEM is a grid of elevation points that describes the terrain. A DEM can be used to derive contours, interpolate percentages of slope, determine the aspect of each slope face, and calculate views. Each viewshed is computed from a given viewing point, which is given parameters such as viewing height, vertical angle of vision, and horizontal angle of vision. The resulting viewshed is the two-dimensional map of all areas that are visible from that viewing point. Several critical viewsheds can be combined to locate areas of high visibility.

In order to study a view that includes existing trees, one must prepare a modified DEM. Heights representing the distance to the top of the dominant vegetation are added to the ground elevations. One height may be added for wooded areas, while a lesser height might be used for orchards. Where the woods end, the computer reads a vertical wall representing the edge of the mass of trees. Each mass of trees interrupts the view to the ground plane beyond. Likewise, rolling terrain can block views to objects in the valleys and on the backsides of ridges.

This map shows the areas visible from Olana's front porch and those hidden from view. The visible areas are shown in a red, horizontal hatch pattern, the invisible areas are shown with a pattern of light blue squares.

A porch with a view

Only one viewing point was used in this study: the view from the front porch of Olana, facing south. The viewshed from the front porch was completed using the ArcInfo viewshed operator. The Saratoga Associates modified a DEM to emulate a ground plane including the heights of existing wooded areas, orchards, and grasslands. The modified DEM allowed for land hidden by trees, and thus suitable for new building, to be identified.

Working with CLC staff, The Saratoga Associates then looked at a second situation: the view without trees, as if developers had clear-cut the land as part of each construction project. This condition makes lands beyond the clear-cut more visible, as are buildings. CLC staff ground-checked parcels with reverting vegetation, as depicted on maps and aerial photographs.

This map demonstrates the extent to which tree cover protects the view from Olana.

Testing for visual intrusions

The lands invisible from Olana's front porch were then tested to see where 35-foot-high potential houses could be located without intruding in the view. The grid of blue squares represents potential parcels. An ArcInfo script was used to simulate a house at each location on the 200-foot grid, shown above on the invisible lands. The model also shows lands already developed (red squares within the red hatch) and excludes wetlands protected by the State of New York (in green).

Where any portion of a house would be visible, a red square replaces the blue one on the map. The result is a map showing where houses can be built without interfering with the view from Olana: all the blue squares.

Viewsheds in action

This study was developed to help the State, Friends of Olana, and land trusts like Scenic Hudson and the Columbia Land Conservancy in their efforts to work with individual, willing landowners to discuss conservation easements.

The viewshed maps also show 1-, 2-, 3-, and 4-mile radii from the Olana view point, as well as local streets. Parcel boundaries can also be shown to help towns identify locations for proposed building.

There are several advantages of using GIS for projects of this type. It is very difficult to calculate viewsheds manually or with the cross-section tool of CADD. You can take photos from the viewing point, but pinpointing visible areas at the extremes of visibility is too difficult to make an accurate map of the viewing extent. The cross-section method is time consuming and does not allow the designer to view natural conditions and political boundaries simultaneously with the viewshed.

Virtually any proposed development, from houses to commercial developments to landfills, can be tested in a viewshed. GIS is clearly the tool of choice for this type of evaluation. Wherever an important viewing point exists, GIS can be used to add a viewshed analysis to the project.

Protection of views from the front porch of Olana was the mission of The Saratoga Associates.

Acknowledgments

Thanks to Lisa Nagle and Dan Wojcik of The Saratoga Associates, Saratoga Springs, New York, and to Ken Grudens of Columbia Land Conservancy, Inc.

Chapter 3

On the edge

THE FRONT RANGE OF THE ROCKY MOUNTAINS is where the grassy plains of the country's midsection merge with the slopes of the Continental Divide. It is where westward migrations first encountered the most treacherous of passages, and it is where many decided to take root. It is still an appealing place for natives and newcomers alike. The area's natural beauty, its proximity to year-round recreation, and its thriving economy have made the front range a developer's paradise.

One spot along the front range undergoing phenomenal growth is Commerce City, Colorado. Until recently it was a small, predominantly industrial town. At the outer edge of Denver, with comparatively low property values and flat land for easy construction, Commerce City was an attractive location for light manufacturing companies. The city that took its name from its primary activity had a daytime population double that of its tax-paying residents, who numbered about 18,000. With the construction of the new Denver International Airport and the E-470 beltway, all that changed. What was once an outlying suburb has become the gateway to metropolitan Denver.

Commerce City seized the opportunity for growth and annexed 43 square miles of Adams County. This increased the area under its jurisdiction by 400 percent. Anticipating development pressure due to its proximity to the new airport, improved access to downtown Denver, and new, vacant lands, the city moved decisively. Instead of letting development take its course, Commerce City, including its Department of Parks, Recreation, and Golf, commissioned several planning studies.

City officials then sought a way to use all these studies in their daily planning and permitting activities. Enter the design team led by Urban Edges, greenway planners; DHM Design, landscape architects; and Tuttle Applegate, engineers.

Photographs by Urban Edges

Commerce City is taking steps to grow wisely.

A GIS atlas

In response to the city's request, the pitch made by the Urban Edges team was for an interactive parks and planning atlas to be used by all the city's departments. The atlas would be used to test the fit of each proposal in the fabric of both the existing and future communities. All projects currently moving through the planning pipeline would be shown on the atlas, along with their completion status. The atlas would be used not only to review proposals, but also to make suggestions for revisions. Design guidelines included with the atlas demonstrate to developers the specific character of desirable improvements in Commerce City. High on the city's list

of appropriate improvements are preservation of open space and provisions for recreation and wildlife habitat.

The atlas compiled the results of more than a dozen planning studies, including the Commerce City Parks & Recreation Master Plan (prepared by EDAW) and The New Lands Comprehensive Plan (prepared by BRW). The adjacent Rocky Mountain Arsenal National Wildlife Refuge added another 17 square miles to the study area. Even though Commerce City currently has no authority there, the city will be taking possession of approximately 900 acres, of which 200 acres will

become a new community park. The Rocky Mountain Arsenal Wildlife Refuge Management Plan (prepared by Design Workshop) was incorporated in the atlas and used for tying trails and wildlife corridors in the city to those in the refuge. Results of studies from several adjacent cities, as well as county and state entities, were also included in the atlas. A complete list of the adjoining corridors is shown as a table, and these are delineated on the overall Prairieways Plan. The various planning recommendations were brought together to form a master plan report entitled "Commerce City Prairieways Plan."

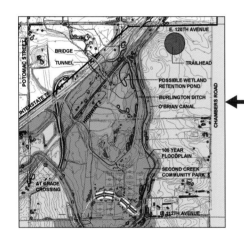

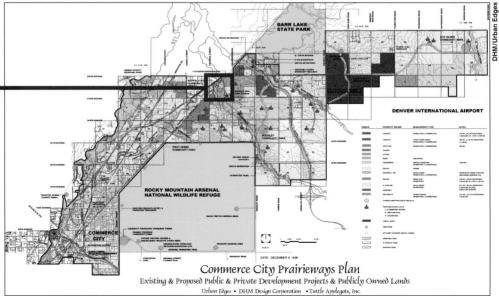

The atlas key map shows how the 65-mile-square sections cover the study area. Electronic links from each section, or plate, to projects within it streamline planning sessions.

Planning and management standards

Along with compilation of the various plan proposals, Urban Edges and DHM Design organized the recreation standards and design guidelines from the disparate reports into concise lists of selection and design criteria. Planning and management standards were also articulated in the Action Plan. Everything the planners in the various city departments need for reviewing development proposals and educating those involved was provided in the atlas and the Action Plan.

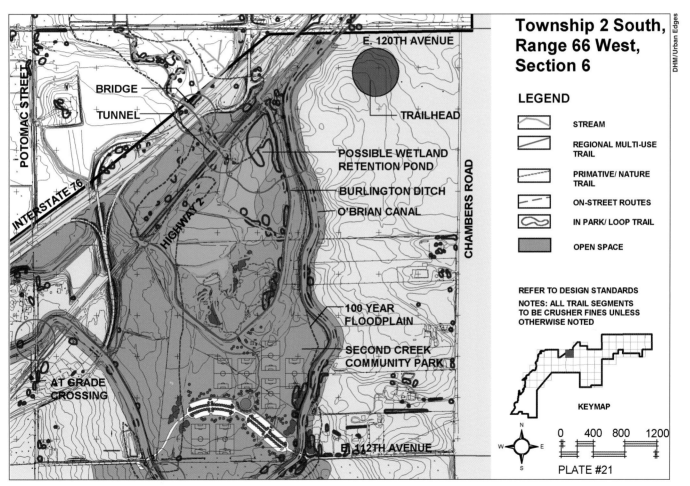

Plate 21 shows the site plan for Second Creek Community Park, a facility with seven basketball courts.

Sixty-five sections, one master plan

The atlas also includes raw GIS data: topography, soils, vegetation, drainage, flood hazard, ownership, and aerial photos. Early in the study, data had been purchased from Harrison Data Sets of Fort Collins, Colorado. Later, much of this data was enhanced by DHM Design. The GIS data provided the information at the master plan resolution, covering the sixty-five 1-square-mile, tiled sections. Since Commerce City is an ArcView GIS user, all the GIS data was prepared in ArcView GIS.

Nested within the sixty-five sections of the master plan are detailed plans for individual parks, greenways, or trails. Data was supplied for the unit plans by the Adams County Public Works Department from AutoCAD® files projected to State Plane coordinates. This projection gives all the overlying themes the reference they need to line up properly with one another. The information provided at the site scale included topography, utilities, streets and curbs, ownership, zoning, vegetation, and flood hazards.

Some of the parks and recreation areas proposed by the earlier planning studies had conceptual site plans, others did not. Referring to the combined master plan, and checking for accuracy in trail linkages, wildlife corridors, park type designations (neighborhood, community, or regional), and fulfillment of recreation demand, the team completed and modified the individual site plans.

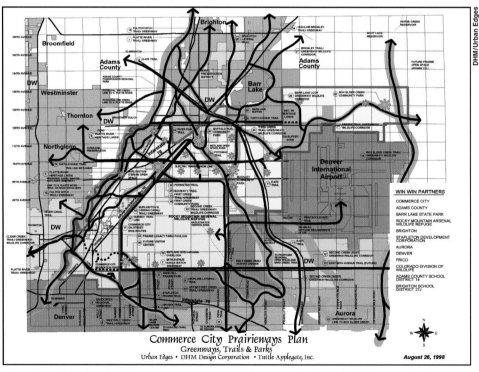

This schematic master plan shows open space and recreation proposals throughout Commerce City.

The atlas architecture

During the development review process, city staff will frequently be moving back and forth from the citywide master plan to the plates to the individual recreation site plans. In order to simplify these transitions, a nesting structure was developed. Each of the individual site plans was linked to the section(s) in which it resides. Most of the sixty-five sections have a numbered hot link, which when activated on the computer screen pulls up the conceptual site plan for that section, including any planned parks, open spaces, and trails. This hot link scheme was made possible by the script-writing skills of the people at DHM Design. Ternary Spatial Research (TSR) was then engaged to develop a graphical interface for input of proposals by the various agency staffs and for research by the public.

Text describing each unit's design concept, critical characteristics of each site, essential design features, and certain quantity take-offs are also linked to the master plan. The raw GIS data maps, especially topography, drainage, and ownership, can help staff make decisions about changes to the unit plans. The Action Plan report also includes a chapter on design guidelines so that reviewing staff can see the intent of the whole recreation system as well as features within the units. The Action Plan is a tool kit as much as it is a master plan.

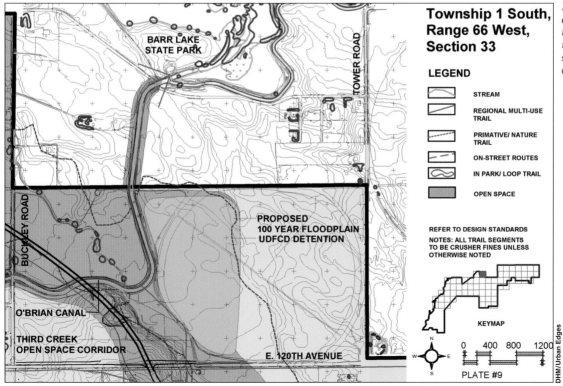

In addition to site plans for existing and proposed parks, the design guidelines state minimum development standards and management objectives.

A day in the life

During the plan review process, city staff will locate the developer's proposal on the citywide master plan. Each proposal will fall within one or more of the 1-square-mile sections or plates. Detailed information for that section can be viewed on the computer screen by calling up the relevant GIS themes. If there are recreation facilities within the section, the staff will activate the hot link to the site plan and the design criteria by clicking on the number for that facility. The hot link will bring up the CAD drawing of the conceptual site plan and the text related to that site's design concept. The drawings and text may be printed, or simply examined on-screen as agency staff and the developer discuss the proposal.

Making improvements

When making recommendations for significant changes to adjacent recreation facilities, the developer may hire a landscape architect in order to refine the proposal. If the proposed change is minor, the staff person may modify the plan on the computer. Periodically, an experienced designer will review the unit plans and changes will be reflected in the citywide master plan.

Just as development plans may affect park designs, staff members may similarly recommend changes to the developer's proposal. These suggestions may help to improve trail connections, enhance greenway integrity, reduce flood potential, modify views, or respond to recreation needs.

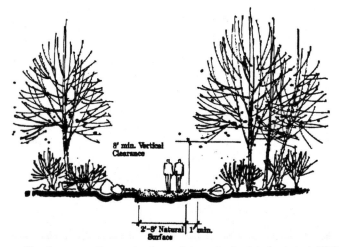

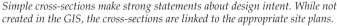

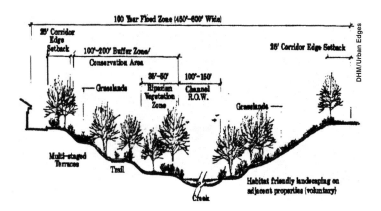

Simple cross-sections make strong statements about design intent. While not created in the GIS, the cross-sections are linked to the appropriate site plans.

The way of the future

Several aspects of this study are unique to places like Commerce City; several are unique to planning and design in 1999.

Because much of the area is undeveloped, consistent guidelines can be applied, making it much easier and less costly to develop an integrated greenway, trail, and park system.

Since most of the study area falls under the jurisdiction of a single government entity, less coordination between agencies is necessary. However, the interactive atlas lends itself to cooperation and information sharing between agencies.

The interactive nature of the atlas and the easy availability of the Action Plan guidelines allow planners and developers to finish reviews much more quickly. By authorizing certain members of its staff to make small modifications to the recreation site designs, Commerce City is able to avoid costly submittals and lengthy reviews.

Commerce City has designated one person to keep the parcel maps current. This provides tremendous advantages in coordinating permits and utilities installation. It saves money for the developers and the city alike.

Changes to the individual park plans do not automatically update the overall recreation master plan. Experienced landscape architects or land planners will review the full master plan periodically so that the cumulative list of recreation amenities is given a holistic inspection.

The days of static master plans are numbered. Designers and developers already rely on the Internet for information. Action plans and online atlases will streamline future urban growth.

The end result of all the planning—people enjoying nature.

Photograph by Urban Edges

Acknowledgments

Thanks to the following:

Rob Thames, Superintendent of Parks,
and Tom Acre, Projects Coordinator,
Commerce City Parks, Recreation,
and Golf

Robert Searns, Lead Planner,
Urban Edges, Denver, Colorado

Bill Neumann, Landscape Architect,
Mark Wilcox, Landscape Architect, and
Bruce Soehngen, GIS Implementation
and Coordination,
DHM Design Corporation,
Denver, Colorado

Dan Giroux, Project Engineer,
Tuttle Applegate Engineers,
Denver, Colorado

Quint Redmond, GIS Specialist,
Ternary Spatial Research (TSR),
Denver, Colorado

Chapter 4

Celebrate the season

SPRING IN SOUTH KOREA is a celebration of peach and cherry and apricot blossoms. Flowers enhance spring parties and picnics announcing Arbor Day, Buddha's Birthday, and Tano, the planting of the crops. Summer brings ceremonies for Farmers Day, Memorial Day, Constitution Day, and Liberation Day. Confucian celebrations fill the fall: Chusok (harvest moon) and Han'gul (the 1446 creation of the alphabet). In winter, Dongji marks the solstice, while the Lunar New Year in February is the most important event of the year.

The owners of the Tae Ah Development Company want their guests to enjoy all of these events at their resort in Kangwon Province. As the lead design firm for the resort, EDAW, Inc., was tasked with finding ways to entice visitors in every month of the year. For year-round enjoyment, resort facilities will include golf, horseback riding, tennis, swimming, hiking, picnicking, alpine skiing, snowboarding, and ice skating. For year-round convenience, accommodations will be clustered in quaint villages. One set of EDAW's plans calls for permanent residents living in condominiums, while in another, overnight guests stay in cabins and townhouses. In both proposals, the smaller units will be in village settings in the subvalleys linked to the central valley. A central village will feature facilities such as restaurants, theaters, galleries, a conference center, shops, a bank, a post office, a day-care center, and a clinic.

Seasonal ceremonies in South Korea traditionally occur in one's home town, but can take on new meaning at a resort.

A hilly retreat

The site is quite dramatic: 2,000 acres of steep hillsides and narrow valleys, opening to the east. The native vegetation is second-growth woodland, with abandoned agricultural fields in the flat areas. The site is high in the watershed where the rugged beauty highlights internal site views. A stream bisects the site from west to east.

In order to increase visitors' appreciation of their mountain setting, all guests will become pedestrians upon arrival. From the formal entry road, guests pull into an underground garage where they will leave their cars for their entire visit. Shuttle vans will move people and their gear from hotels to ski lifts, first tees, and back again.

The site is designed according to the Korean belief in the four cardinal directions plus the center. The Korean designation for north is a black turtle, for east a blue dragon, for south a sunbird, and for west, three white tigers. Thus, there will be four residential villages named Black Turtle, Blue Dragon, Sun Bird, and Three White Tigers around the main village. Other, more remote, villages will provide permanent housing for staff.

At the center of the residential villages will be the main village offering entertainment, culture, and recreation. This central village will be named for a familiar sight in the heavens known in Korea as the seven stars. Seven plazas will lead visitors through the village, which is designed to accommodate day use as well as overnight guests.

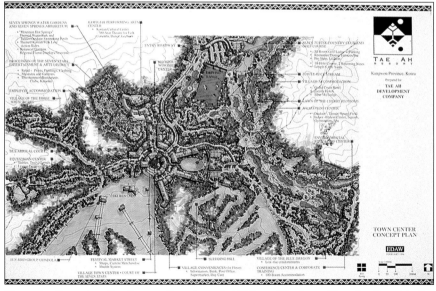

Occupying the main valley, the resort's center, called Village of the Seven Stars, is adjacent to the ski lifts, golf course, and two of the residential villages. Pedestrian walks and shuttle routes link the subvalleys.

Keep it simple

EDAW used only two raw data themes: land cover, derived from an aerial photo, and digital contours, provided by the owner, from which aspect, hillshade (see sidebar), and slope were derived. All the suitability analyses were completed from these two raw data themes.

The rationale behind this GIS model is as follows: to be as economically viable as possible, winter utility use must be minimized. Heating the buildings and making snow for the ski runs are among the biggest winter costs. The easiest way to minimize these costs is to locate ski runs on north-facing slopes, where natural and man-made snow will last longer, and to place most buildings on south-facing slopes, where they will get more sun.

Ski slopes were located with a simple model of slope and aspect. Those slopes below 8 percent are not steep enough for skiing and were eliminated. Slopes 8 to 25 percent are suitable for beginning skiers. Slopes 25 to 40 percent are ideal for intermediate skiers, while 40- to 70-percent slopes will challenge advanced skiers. Anything over 70 percent was also eliminated. Each of these slope categories was then designated as primary or secondary according to its aspect; true north slopes (NNW and NNE) were given prime candidacy, while the slightly warmer slopes (WNW and ENE) were secondary candidates.

SOLAR INTENSITY

The GIS term *hillshade* describes a combination of aspect and slope. Since flatter slopes receive more solar radiation than steeper slopes, hillshade can be calculated to find warmer areas of a site. To create a hillshade theme, those slopes under 8 percent (or some similar value) are given a premium over steeper slopes. Slope is then combined with aspect to find the warmest and coolest places on a site, or the brightest and darkest ones. Because a GIS includes the site's position on the earth as part of its basic information, it is also possible to select a given day of the year and hour of the day for which to calculate sun angle.

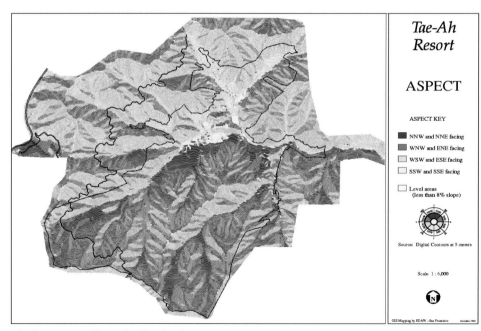

The flat areas usually read as "no data" on aspect maps.

The model

The model for building locations at Tae Ah used the two themes of slope and hillshade. Hillshade was computed for the three winter months, and the worst condition, on the 21st of December, was incorporated into the final analysis. Those areas in sun most of the day were given a higher ranking than those with some shady hours. The slope categories for development included 0 to 15 percent for large buildings and high-density construction, and 15 to 25 percent for townhouse and cabin construction.

The entire site was then divided into the zone north of the stream (facing south) and the zone south of the stream (facing north). The suitability map for ski slopes was pasted into the south zone and the suitability map for development was pasted into the north zone.

The result includes the three levels of ski slopes, with primary and secondary recommendations, and development suitability for large and small units. The property boundary is shown with a dash/dot line; an existing road and an existing highway in the western areas of the map are shown as double lines.

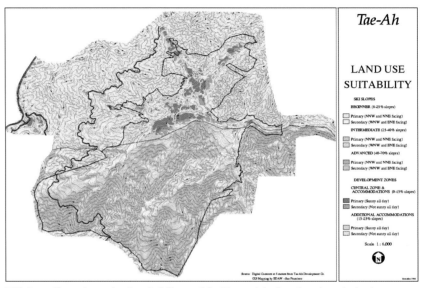

This is a collage of two simple suitability models. The models show locations for beginner (116 acres), intermediate (44 acres), and advanced (237 acres) ski slopes, as well as appropriate zones for high-density (48 acres) and low-density (42 acres) development. GIS reports the quantities shown on output maps automatically.

Landscape architects using GIS for site design

This is a very straightforward use of GIS, with a limited number of issues. Landscape architects are most comfortable in the realm of graphics and spatial concepts, less so in a technical or mathematical setting. The categories shown on the Tae Ah map are readily understood; no decoding is required. Rather than letting the technology force them into unfamiliar ways of working, landscape architects can use GIS in familiar ways.

Acknowledgments

Thanks to David Blau and Peter Jonas of EDAW, Inc., San Francisco, California.

Chapter 5

Subtle beauty

THOSE VISITING FROM THE FORESTED EAST COAST, the tree-rich Midwest, or the lush Northwest, might not appreciate the slight, seasonal variations in color, or the delicate fragrance of the various types of sage scrub and chaparral that are native to southern California. But once you have lived there, you become attached to the stark beauty of yucca candles in bloom, and their sharp contrast with smooth, beige rock outcrops. Those landscapes that are still pristine must be guarded because once damaged, regeneration is slow and painful.

San Diego County's population has more than doubled in the last decade, which has made the disposal of waste increasingly difficult. Once-remote areas of the county, where landfills could be discreetly tucked away, are now inhabited by suburbanites who have moved "to the country" and are adamant about limiting pollution, visual degradation, noise, and traffic congestion.

Gregory Canyon Landfill, near the town of Pala, has been in the design phase for more than ten years. Initially, San Diego County used its discretionary powers to review proposals by the landfill owners themselves. Over the years, members of the community have organized to demand formal environmental reviews. This gave landscape architects an opportunity to study several alternate proposals, making sure that the landfill's visibility would be limited as the landfill takes shape.

Gregory Canyon Landfill is located in northern San Diego County near the town of Pala.

GIS for visual impact

From the beginning, the landscape architecture firm of KTU+A chose to use GIS for the visual impact analyses of the Environmental Impact Reports (EIRs), and for communicating with the local citizens. In its early studies of Gregory Canyon, KTU+A used the ARC GRID™ module of ArcInfo, but in 1998 it used ArcView GIS and the ArcView Spatial Analyst and 3D Analyst extensions to generate viewshed maps and visibility analyses. San Diego County has excellent GIS data, some available through the data clearinghouse at the San Diego Association of Governments (SANDAG).

The portion of the EIR that the landscape architects provided in each new round of the project was the visual analysis. The prime consultant for the EIR was the environmental firm of David Evans and Associates, Inc. The study area includes about 4,000 acres, while the property owned by Gregory Canyon, Limited, covers approximately 1,800 acres, of which the landfill and stockpiles will cover about 350 acres.

Demystifying the subjective

If beauty is in the eye of the beholder, then how objective can visual impact studies be? The purpose of visibility studies is to identify the areas from which people will see the landfill, and to determine how much they will see. Several methods have been developed over the past three decades to provide consistency in visual assessments of the landscape. These methods have been widely employed by the U.S. Forest Service (USFS), the Bureau of Land Management (BLM), and the Federal Highways Administration (FHWA). The Environmental Impact Report was completed under guidelines established by the California Environmental Quality Act (CEQA), which includes standards for visual assessment. KTU+A combined the visual standards outlined by these agencies and added some of its own techniques.

Visual jargon

Several concepts are fairly constant throughout visual analyses. The concept of visual character is defined by the landscape(s) under consideration. Character definitions can include the parameters of scale, color, texture, transient qualities, integrity, variety, and typical landscape elements. The character is unique to each region or landscape unit. Landscape units can be defined as having a consistent character and well-defined boundaries.

Visual quality is usually a rating of how close the scene is to the ideal for that landscape unit. How pristine is the view? How good is this example of Sierra foothills? How far does this scene diverge from the perfect oak savanna? Quality ratings often include measures for man-made structures, which can reinforce the scene, be of little consequence in the view, or seriously diminish the quality of the view.

Visibility ratings can be quite objective: either you see it or you do not. The visibility rating is the measure of how many times certain areas are seen from all the possible viewing points, or from selected ones. GIS identifies and counts these views quite efficiently.

A viewshed is the two-dimensional map of all areas visible from a given point at a given height. Composite viewsheds identify all the areas that are seen from one viewing point, those that are visible from two points, and so forth. These composite viewshed maps give a quantifiable measure of visibility. The query function can be used to give a report in acres or square feet of each category of visibility.

Whether viewsheds are being generated for visual assessment as part of an EIR, or as part of the site analysis for design, the viewpoints should be those to which users will have frequent access, and from which they will see significant existing or potential views. One of the advantages of constructing viewsheds within the computer is that you need not place yourself at the viewpoint in the field. Getting to the viewpoint in the field can be difficult in treacherous terrain, with unfriendly landowners, in bad weather, or simply when time is short. Since the computer allows you to select the existing grade elevation, or an imaginary "z" factor, you can also test the viewshed from a second- or third-story window not yet in existence.

Visual sensitivity, also called visual absorption, is an indication of the ability of the landscape to withstand development without loss of quality. A numeric rating is normally assigned indicating a low, moderate, or high sensitivity. A landscape with a low sensitivity rating can absorb a lot of development without losing its quality. A high sensitivity rating means the area is very susceptible to change and will lose its quality with minor development. Conversely, a high visual absorption rating means that the landscape unit can withstand a lot of development without losing its quality.

Distance zones are usually described as foreground, middle ground, background, and seldom seen. There is much debate over the exact boundaries of these zones, but one reference identifies foreground as being within the nearest quarter mile, and background as starting 2 miles from the viewer (Smardon, et al., 1986). The rationale for identifying distance zones is that elements of the same size make a bigger impact in the foreground than in the middle ground, and so forth.

I have developed a method that I call the bovine method. If cows are visible in your view, and you can distinguish their ears, they are in the foreground. If you cannot make out their ears, but you can see their legs, they are in the middle ground. When legs are no longer discernible, they are in the background. The method works on horses, deer, and elk as well.

Visual simulations are graphic images that resemble views of the proposal after installation. Before computers, simulations were done as collages on photographs. Nowadays, CAD drawings of buildings, roadways, landscape structures, and contours can be transformed into three-dimensional views in a GIS showing both existing conditions and proposed improvements. An exaggerated vertical dimension can be used to heighten the effect of grading operations. Aerial photos can be superimposed on the terrain to give a realistic view of the area, and graphics can be drawn to indicate proposed use zones and circulation patterns.

Defining the site

In order to evaluate conditions in 2027, at the completion of the landfill, KTU+A modified a digital elevation model. The original DEM was supplied by the U.S. Geological Survey and imported into the GIS. The civil engineers for the project, Bryan A. Stirrat & Associates, provided contours of the finished landfill as AutoCAD DWG files, which were used to modify the DEM. This finished surface was used to calculate all the viewsheds and visibility studies.

Who sees what?

KTU+A first determined how visible the landfill and its support facilities (borrow pit and fill stockpile) would be. There are two primary populations of viewers: those who live nearby and will view the landfill from their homes, and those who drive on Highway 76.

The first visibility study calculated viewsheds looking from the landfill into the surrounding communities. After calculating fifty viewsheds from different points on the finished landfill, KTU+A prepared a composite viewshed, shown here with five levels of visibility. Views to the landfill from the neighborhoods were computed and revealed that the North Hillside community will view the greatest number of points on the landfill. The firm further did an analysis of the potential number of residential viewers by estimating the maximum number of future homes, based on zoning densities for each residential area.

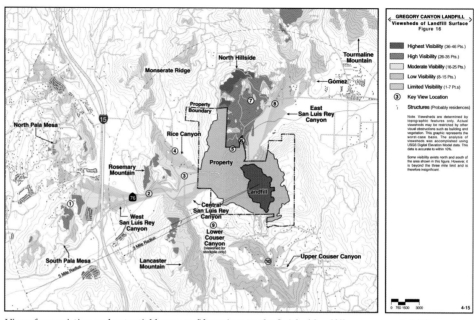

Views from existing and potential homes to fifty points on the finished landfill were computed. Those areas shown in red and orange have the highest visibility of the finished landfill, while only small portions of it can be seen from the blue areas.

Taking the scenic route

Travelers on Highway 76 will also view the landfill as they drive through the valley. KTU+A used field surveys to record the number of seconds motorists would view the landfill while traveling at a speed of 40 miles per hour in either direction.

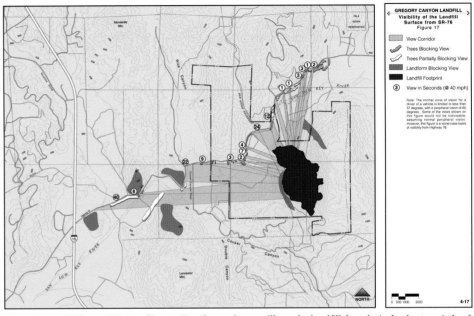

Motorists on Highway 76, traveling at 40 miles per hour, will see the landfill for relatively short periods of time. Twenty-four seconds is the longest viewing time at close range.

How scenic is it?

An early step in the process was the assign-
ment of visual quality and visual sensitivity ratings for the immediate surroundings
of the landfill. About 2,000 acres were
divided into twenty-one distinguishable
landscape units. Standard rating forms
developed by the FHWA were used for
each of the twenty-one landscape units to
assess the visual quality and visual sensitivity. The results of the quality and sensitivity assessments were then combined
with the results of the visibility studies
described above to form the visual resource
classifications established by the BLM. The
composite Visual Resource Classifications
map is shown here and includes Class II,
III, and IV ratings.

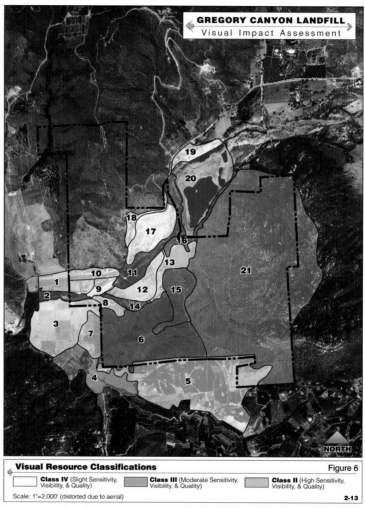

*The Bureau of Land Management developed the standards for this Visual
Resource Classifications map.*

Can mitigation help?

One of the purposes of an EIR, besides determining the impacts of the proposed action, is to recommend mitigating measures. KTU+A took photos in the field, then examined the photos and the visibility studies to identify ten key viewpoints in the study area. These photos were then used as the bases to simulate various visual mitigation measures (VMM). The landscape architects recommended a variety of visual barriers, such as tree masses and earth berms.

Ten VMMs were proposed and evaluated, including vegetative screening of the landfill, screening with landforms, blending landfill finish grades with the surrounding grades, placement of rock outcrops on the finished landfill, tree plantings to blend finished landfill surface with its surroundings (this also reinforces nonvisual habitat mitigation measures), plantings of native shrubs and plants (for the same results provided by trees), texture matching with plants and rocks, adjustments to engineering structures, and adjustments to the footprint or finished height of the landfill.

An example of the visual simulations is shown here. The VMM shown in this simulation is trees planted in the foreground to hide the finished landfill. Simulations of this type are very effective in communicating with the client and the public and can be used to test and refine alternatives.

The ArcView GIS 3D Analyst extension was used to generate three-dimensional views of the actual midterm and completed ground surfaces. These 3-D views were adjusted to match the viewing angle and sun angle shown in each of the photographs taken at the ten key points. The photographs were scanned into Adobe® Photoshop® and the GIS 3-D views were imported as JPEG images.

Each landfill terrain was then fitted onto the appropriate photograph along with simulations of VMM. This approach results in accurate visualizations of the proposals and very realistic images.

Each of the simulation studies includes a viewshed map locating the key viewpoint, a photo of the existing condition, a photo simulation of the view after fifteen years of landfill operation, a simulation of the view after thirty years of operation without mitigation, and a simulation of the finished landfill with proposed mitigation measures.

Measuring the amount of change

KTU+A then developed its own rating method to evaluate the visual characteristics of each of these simulations. Entitled "Degree of Contrast," the evaluation forms were used to rate the amount of change from the existing condition, to the condition during the build-up of the landfill, to the condition at completion of the landfill without mitigation, and finally, to the finished landfill with mitigation measures. Each of these key views was evaluated for five types of changes: form, line, texture, contrast (color and value), and character (variety and unity). The simulation ratings also considered improvements such as new roads and bridges. The question was then asked, "Does the mitigated proposal meet resource management objectives?"

A rating of 0 was given for no contrast with existing conditions, 1 for weak contrast, 2 for moderate, and 3 for strong. The total scores could range from 0 to 15, and were summarized as Type 1, 2, or 3.

KTU+A's contrast ratings showed that some of the finished grading should be modified. These suggested changes were analyzed to see if they did, in fact, lower the visibility or decrease the contrast. Multiple viewshed maps were generated to confirm reduced visibility. The new viewshed maps were used in conversations with the civil engineers, who reshaped certain areas of the finished landfill surface, making it less visible.

GIS in visual assessment

In recent years, many powerful programs have been developed for visualizing three-dimensional projects based on CAD drawings. Small-scale simulations of mitigation measures have improved with new rendering and lighting programs. In the rush to use these extremely sophisticated 3-D products, GIS has often been overlooked.

The Gregory Canyon Landfill Visual Analysis makes good use of GIS in studying the visual quality of the study area and in identifying the neighborhoods most affected by the proposal. Visual analysis is one of the components of environmental documents that is rightfully the domain of landscape architects. Much work remains in protecting our visual resources, and GIS will play an important role in research, demonstration, and design.

Suggested readings

Smardon, Richard C., James F. Palmer and John P. Felleman, editors, 1986, *Foundations for Visual Project Analysis,* New York, John Wiley & Sons, Inc.

U.S. Department of Agriculture, Forest Service, 1974, *The Visual Management System, National Forest Landscape Management Volume 2*

Hornbeck, Peter L. and Garland A. Okerlund, Jr., 1973, *Visual Values for the Highway User,* Federal Highway Administration

Remy, Michael H., Tina A. Thomas and James G. Moore, 1995, *Guide to California Environmental Quality Act (CEQA),* Solana Press

Acknowledgments

Thanks to Mark Carpenter of KTU+A, San Diego, California.

Chapter 6

A monument to the American West

IT IS NOT OFTEN THAT ONE IS ENTRUSTED to protect a national treasure, but that is what the City of Colorado Springs Water Resources Department has done for eight decades. The department manages the south watershed of Pikes Peak, the mountain that forms the backdrop to the city of Colorado Springs. As the population of the region has grown, its guardianship has become ever more vigilant. At the end of the century the department has the task of keeping 600,000 eager outdoor enthusiasts at bay. The pressure to invade the watershed has become intense.

The site sits in stunning Colorado mountain country. At 14,110 feet, Pikes Peak is not the tallest in the state, but only one of 54 peaks that exceed 14,000 feet in elevation. Its southern watershed contains many historic mines, Mueller State Park, rare species found nowhere else on earth, and fabulous views in all seasons. This 200-square-mile watershed is a pristine canvas waiting to be marked by anxious recreationists.

It is not often that landscape architects get to work on a national treasure either, but Design Workshop got that opportunity in 1998. Pressure was mounting to open up the watershed, and the Water Resources Department knew they could not hold off that pressure forever. The department called for a sustainable land-use plan for the watershed that was widely supported by the community. What the Water Resources Department liked about Design Workshop's approach was its detailed proposal to involve the community throughout the decision-making process, and its technical strategy to safeguard critical resources.

Aspens and evergreens blanket Pikes Peak, along with layers of snow. Recreationists are eager to explore and exploit its natural beauty.

Increasing participation

A diverse group of local resource planners was organized as technical advisors, giving the project greater credibility with the nearby communities. Products of the technical strategy included opportunity maps, showing locations for activities suggested by the citizens, and a carrying capacity analysis measuring impacts of recreation uses on the various natural resources.

To begin the planning process, the Water Department initiated a coalition of fourteen partners: all governmental agencies with a stake in the watershed were involved. The managing partners included administrators and/or staff of the Water Resources Department of the City of Colorado Springs, the U.S. Forest Service (Pike and San Isabel National Forests), the Pikes Peak Division of Colorado State Highways, the City of Green Mountain Falls, representatives of the Ute Nation, the Colorado Department of State Parks, the Colorado Division of Wildlife, the City of Cripple Creek, El Paso County, the Bureau of Land Management, the Town of Victor, the City of Manitou Springs, the City of Woodland Park, and Teller County.

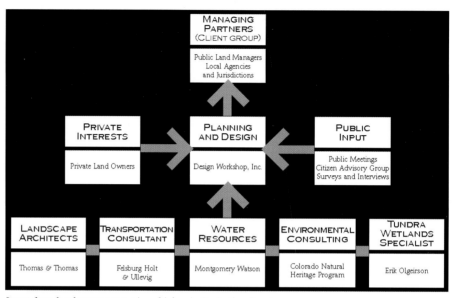

Input from local groups was given high priority in the planning process.

Public participation

A citizens' advisory group was formed to provide input and continuity throughout the planning period, and open forums were held in the surrounding communities as well. Throughout the project, a newsletter called *Peak Views* regularly updated the community on progress. Further, a Web site provided a digital link to the design team. No one in the community could complain about being left out of this process.

Design Workshop used print, a Web site, and face-to-face meetings to inform citizens and ask for input.

Describing the desired results

There were three primary goals to be achieved through the design process: produce a solution based on a multiuse vision derived from common community values; find common management strategies for the entire ecosystem, regardless of ownership; and balance the use of the available resources.

Subordinate objectives included restoring and maintaining the health of the ecosystem, matching activity programs to the land's carrying capacity, clearly defining resource management objectives, developing a plan with a high level of public support, developing effective public/private partnerships, implementing an affordable plan, protecting water quality, conserving and perpetuating the quality of the area's resources, teaching sustainability issues to the public, creating a plan that is consistent across jurisdictions, and developing an environmentally based plan.

Consultant roles

Design Workshop led the design team by developing the community input approach and the technical process. A group of specialists from the Colorado Natural Heritage Program, Colorado State University, and The Nature Conservancy inventoried the plant and animal communities of the watershed. The report they prepared, "Biological Survey of the Pikes Peak Area 1999 Final Report," provided up-to-date baseline data. Subconsultants to Design Workshop included another firm of landscape architects, Thomas and Thomas, which was hired to assess cultural resources. Felsburg, Holt & Ulevig served as the transportation specialists, Montgomery Watson as the water resources engineers, while expertise on tundra and wetlands was provided by Eric Olgerson.

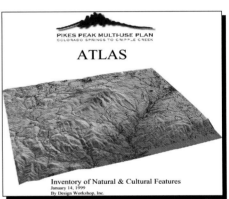

An atlas of GIS maps was presented to the client for their future use.

Moving through the steps

In addition to large public meetings and a series of meetings with various user groups, the process included a written survey distributed throughout the community. Allowing practically everyone to have input, the survey generated a "wish list" of sixty-six types of activities for the watershed, including activities as diverse as agriculture, backpacking, bird watching, back country skiing, bicycle racing, resort vacations, shore fishing, and of course its primary, historic use, water storage.

It had been decided that a geographic information system would be used to provide the data manipulation required by the design team. A GIS atlas was prepared of basemaps, derived maps such as visual analysis and potential wetlands, and aerial photos. The atlas became another product for the communities and the resource managers to use after the study was complete.

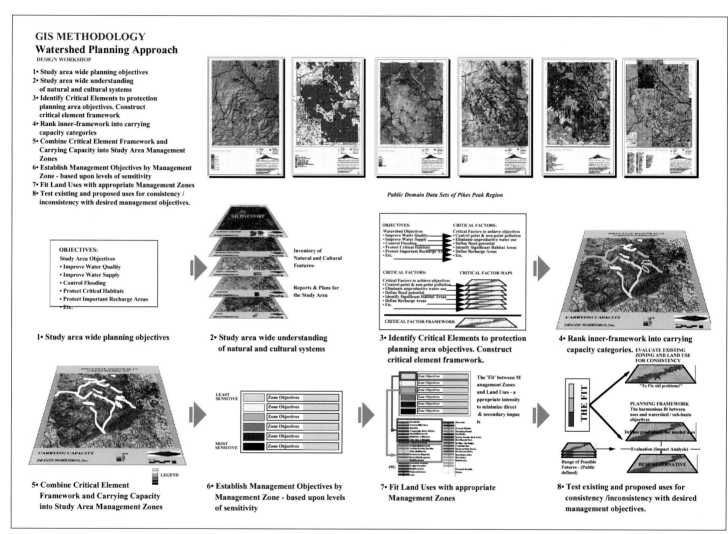

GIS METHODOLOGY
Watershed Planning Approach
DESIGN WORKSHOP

1• Study area wide planning objectives
2• Study area wide understanding
   of natural and cultural systems
3• Identify Critical Elements to protection
   planning area objectives. Construct
   critical element framework
4• Rank inner-framework into carrying
   capacity categories
5• Combine Critical Element Framework and
   Carrying Capacity into Study Area Management
   Zones
6• Establish Management Objectives by Management
   Zone - based upon levels of sensitivity
7• Fit Land Uses with appropriate Management Zones
8• Test existing and proposed uses for consistency /
   inconsistency with desired management objectives.

Public Domain Data Sets of Pikes Peak Region

1• Study area wide planning objectives

2• Study area wide understanding
   of natural and cultural systems

3• Identify Critical Elements to protection
   planning area objectives. Construct
   critical element framework.

4• Rank inner-framework into carrying
   capacity categories.

5• Combine Critical Element
   Framework and Carrying Capacity
   into Study Area Management Zones

6• Establish Management Objectives by
   Management Zone - based upon levels
   of sensitivity

7• Fit Land Uses with appropriate
   Management Zones

8• Test existing and proposed uses for
   consistency /inconsistency with desired
   management objectives.

*In this process diagram, the capacity maps are prepared in steps 2, 3, and 4, the opportunity maps
come from steps 5, 6, and 7, and the alternative future maps are step 8.*

Capacity maps

The fourteen local experts participated in a modified Delphi Method in order to develop the criteria for the opportunity maps and the carrying capacity models. These experts knew the identity of the group members but followed Delphi procedures in expressing their opinions. After each round the questionnaires were sent to the group and the "average" response was identified. When responding to the next round of questions, each member could either accept the "average" response or restate their opinion about the issue. With each round the standard deviation would drop, and once the deviation was below 1 the design team would rule that consensus had been reached. Most issues only required two or three iterations of the process to reach consensus.

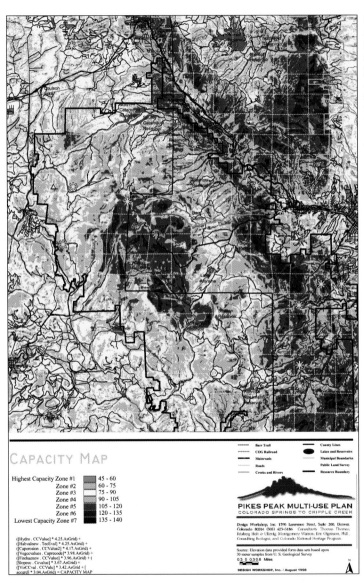

Carrying capacity models generated maps that predicted the impacts of the various proposals. The Technical Advisory Group used a statistically valid process to come to consensus on which maps defined "capacity" and how to weight each map.

CAPACITY MAP

Highest Capacity Zone #1
Zone #2
Zone #3
Zone #4
Zone #5
Zone #6
Lowest Capacity Zone #7

45 - 60
60 - 75
75 - 90
90 - 105
105 - 120
120 - 135
135 - 140

([Hydro . CCValue] * 4.25.AsGrid) +
([Habvalnew . TecEval] * 4.25.AsGrid) +
([Caperosion . CCValue2] * 4.17.AsGrid) +
([Vegecvalues . Caprecode]* 3.98.AsGrid) +
([Firehaznew . CCValue]* 3.96.AsGrid) + (
[Slopece . Cevalue]* 3.67.AsGrid) +
([VisCCval . CCValu]* 3.42.AsGrid + [
accgrd] * 3.04.AsGrid) = CAPACITY MAP

Baer Trail
COG Railroad
Mainroads
Roads
Creeks and Rivers

County Lines
Lakes and Reservoirs
Municipal Boundaries
Public Land Survey
Resource Boundary

PIKES PEAK MULTI-USE PLAN
COLORADO SPRINGS TO CRIPPLE CREEK

Design Workshop, Inc. 1390 Lawrence Street, Suite 200, Denver, Colorado 80204 (303) 623-5186 Consultants: Thomas Thomas, Felsburg Holt & Ullevig; Montgomery Watson; Eric Olgienson, PhD; Consulting Ecologist, and Colorado National Heritage Program.

Source: Elevation data provided form data sets based upon 30 meter samples from U. S. Geological Survey
0 3 0 0.3 0.6 Miles

DESIGN WORKSHOP, Inc. / August 1998

Opportunity maps

Opportunity maps identifying areas of the watershed that would have similar management were prepared in the GIS. The various recreation uses were sited based on the carrying capacity of each zone, as determined by a modified Delphi Method (see sidebar) employed by the local resource managers. The management approach for each zone then became the basis for judging its carrying capacity, or its ability to maintain its integrity while accommodating recreation affects.

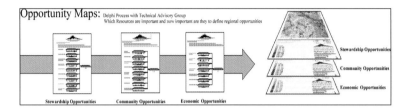

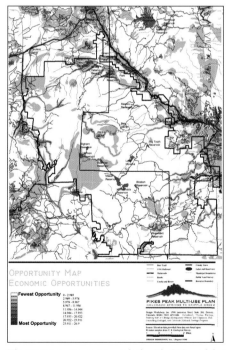

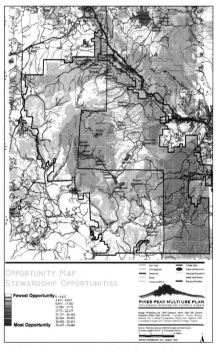

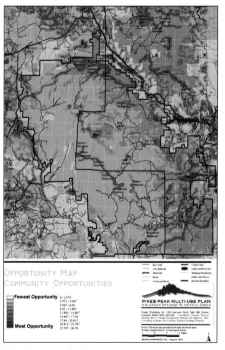

The resource managers worked with GIS models to generate the opportunity maps that located the various uses within the watershed.

Test proposals for management goals

Alternative futures were established during a three-day charette (see sidebar) involving the citizens' advisory group, the heads of all the managing partner agencies, and the design team. Three alternative futures were prepared for consideration at the charette. One plan highlighted environmental protection, one focused on provision of maximum recreation opportunities, and a third represented maximum opportunities for economic development. A "dot test" (see sidebar) was used on the three Alternative Futures as a qualitative review of each proposal. Each participant in the charette was given five green adhesive dots and five red adhesive dots. The green dots were placed on the alternative plans next to features that the citizens supported, and the red dots were placed next to features they did not support. By counting the dots on each of the plans, the design team was able to carry forward the acceptable ideas while eliminating those less acceptable to the citizens' advisory group.

The dot tests employed by the citizens' advisory group were used to form two composite alternatives: an environmental plan combined with recreation facilities and a recreation plan combined with economic elements. These two alternatives represented the best concepts from the original three scenarios, while eliminating the weakest ideas.

The experts evaluated these two combined alternatives for their effects on water resources, environmental resources, cultural resources, and transportation systems. The experts once again used the modified Delphi Method to reach consensus on the carrying capacity of the proposals. The revisions developed as a result of this impact analysis became the final plan for the Pikes Peak region.

In summary, the team's approach put ArcInfo software and GIS to work to: prepare detailed inventories of natural and cultural features; apply locational models to identify the most suitable places for specific uses; apply predictive models

DELPHI METHOD

The Delphi Method was developed to solicit expert opinions while achieving consensus. The Rand Corporation originated the technique to estimate the length of time required to satisfy research goals. In its original form, the experts were anonymous; neither those in the expert group nor those in the general population were aware of the identity of the experts. In Modified Delphi Method, the experts may be known.

Opinions are requested of the experts in series. A statement is made such as, "Over a ten-year period, what is the likelihood that mountain biking will seriously diminish the health of an alpine meadow?" The experts will respond with answers that may range from 100% likelihood to 50% likelihood. To begin the second round, each expert will be given a tally from the first round and asked for a revised opinion. Let us say that the tally of answers from the first round of a group of twenty experts was: 1 said 100%, 3 said 90%, 9 said 80%, 5 said 70% and 2 said 50%. The tally from the next round might look like this: 4 said 90%, 11 said 80%, and 5 said 70%. The requests will continue, always with the knowledge of the answers from the previous round, until there is consensus on the issue.

DOT TESTS

Dot tests, also known as qualitative judgments or group method, are used to limit the number of alternatives being considered. In essence, each participant is allowed to vote for a limited number of items, which represent their preferences. If a community is holding a public meeting using this method to design a park, each citizen will be allowed to vote for an equal number of amenities in the park. The votes will then be tallied and those amenities with the highest number of votes will be included in the design while the others will be eliminated.

to evaluate the impacts of alternative proposals; and set up an ongoing landscape
management system for long-term decision making by the managing partners.

The draft plan was presented to agencies and local municipalities and at public
forums. Comments were taken and a
refined plan, based on expert evaluation
and reflecting community concerns,
was prepared. The multiuse plan report
includes a physical plan, a detailed management plan, and an implementation
strategy to make the vision a reality.
The digital atlas will allow the Water
Resources Department to make adjustments to the final plan as projects are
implemented.

CHARETTE

The term *charette* is used widely in the design fields, and little used outside
them. The origin of the term is French. Teams of design students at the École de
Beaux Arts were assigned design projects that required very intense work of
short duration. The teams would work at studios spread all over Paris and as the
deadline approached, the school sent out a cart (charette) to pick up their
work. Often with dismay, the students would see the charette at their door and
know it was time to surrender their drawings or models.

These days charettes may be as short as one day and as long as a week. Sometimes the hours of participation are designated, at other times participants are
free to work around the clock. All charettes are conducted by teams of designers, experts, and/or citizens, not individuals. The purpose of the charette is to
put pressure on the participants in order to force difficult decisions.

GIS or bust?

What are the advantages of GIS to the
Pikes Peak Multi-Use Plan? Some of the
advantages are common to most site planning projects conducted in a GIS: it is efficient, inclusive, and graphically flexible.
The iterative power of GIS was used to
test alternatives. The GIS was able to
incorporate the objective ratings established by the public and the experts in its
modeling operations. Lastly, the dynamic
nature of the GIS allows the decision-
making process to continue as fine-tuning
is needed.

The Pikes Peak watershed is a dynamic
setting. As the agencies responsible for
its management experience changes in
policies and personnel, the day-to-day
operations will change. As the nearby
communities grow and change in character, recreation demands will change. At
some point the changes will be so great
that the managers will need to begin
again, with a design team making new
judgments about the old models, or
employing new models entirely. In the
meantime, the agencies themselves are
capable of making minor adjustments to
the maps and management recommendations. Master plans are no longer static—
they must live and breathe to be useful.

Acknowledgments

Thanks to Steve Mullens of Design Workshop, Denver, Colorado.

Chapter 7

Classic Americana

ATHENS, GEORGIA, IS ONE OF THOSE FORTUNATE SMALL TOWNS that has maintained the historic character of its downtown. The commercial vitality of the town center is due in part to the quality of its historic buildings and its pedestrian-friendly sidewalks. This is postcard Americana: Norman Rockwell could have slept here.

One of the threats to Athens' small-town feel is Atlanta. Each year metropolitan Atlanta advances 2 to 3 miles along its freeways. The center of Athens is only 70 miles east of the center of Atlanta, and the outer limits of each city are creeping closer and closer. Therefore, one of the major issues is protecting the greenbelt of outer Clarke County through restrictions on development in the rural areas.

The city of Athens occupies a great deal of Clarke County. In order to eliminate redundancies in services, the two entities have formed a consolidated government known as Athens–Clarke County.

Athens nurtures a diverse culture. The area is home to a thriving music business, an aviation tradition, a healthy retail sector, expanding tourism, and a major university. Athens' popularity has resulted in development of many new neighborhoods and infill projects. Land developers and historic preservationists work together to maintain the character of this town.

The previous comprehensive plan was completed in 1994, without the benefit of GIS. In August of 1998, Fregonese Calthorpe Associates (FCA) began preparing a new comprehensive plan, this time using a GIS format. The consolidated

Athens, Georgia, offers the type of small-town atmosphere that cities like Atlanta cannot successfully emulate.

government provided the data, including zoning, vacant land, parcel data, building footprints, pavement areas, digital aerial photos, and natural resources such as floodplains, wetlands, and hydrography. Working closely with the GIS/Graphics Division of the Athens–Clarke County Planning Department, FCA mapped environmental constraints from aerial photos and studied existing land-use patterns, growth patterns, and demographics.

A questionnaire was prepared and distributed through two local newspapers, encouraging public participation. It asked for opinions about rural protection, buffer zones along streams and rivers, redevelopment in the city centers, and increased residential and business development along bus routes. The planners and landscape architects then conducted an extensive cycle of meetings with agency staff, committees, and elected officials. Public

presentations were also made to solicit responses to the initial proposals.

Throughout the project, ad hoc committees met monthly to review and provide reactions to the work. These committees were made up of home builders, bankers, environmental advocates, advocates for historic preservation, and University of Georgia representatives. Monthly reviews were also conducted by the planning commission and the government council.

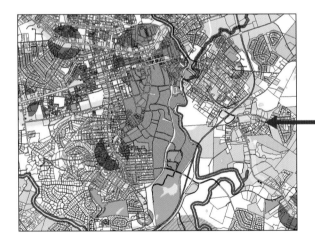

The comprehensive plan addressed urban and rural issues at several scales.

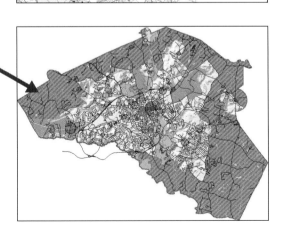

Combining the disciplines

The team then produced a preliminary land-use plan. These land-use proposals were tested against systems such as transportation, environmentally sensitive areas, schools, parks, and special districts. For the transportation impact study, the planners analyzed household and employment projections provided by the client and assigned that data to existing transportation analysis zones. The zone projections were then used as the basis for modeling with a transportation program, EMME2. The results of this model were then imported into ArcView GIS and became part of the land-use plan.

Another impact study identified constrained lands based on conditions such as wetlands (with a 50-foot buffer), open water, riparian corridors (also with a 50-foot buffer), FEMA floodplains, and groundwater recharge areas. The ad hoc environmental committee used the aerial photos to locate these sensitive lands, relying on their personal knowledge of the county. The constrained lands were off limits for land-use proposals.

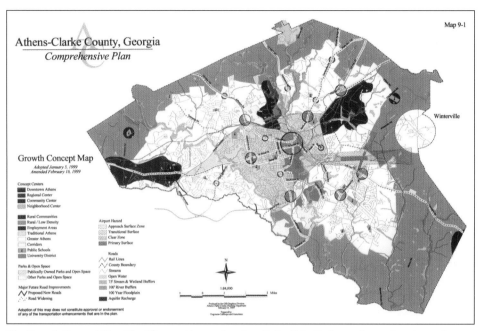

The Growth Concept Plan identifies corridors and centers that will be the focus of new planning and design efforts.

Comparison planning

One of the advantages of GIS is that it quickly measures the amounts of conditions such as constrained lands. The table at the right shows fifteen land-use types with acreages of each. ArcView GIS was used to calculate the areas of each land use and five subcategories indicating status: total, built, vacant, constrained, and vacant unconstrained. This exercise would take days to accomplish with a planimeter but takes minutes to complete in a GIS. No longer should designers be reluctant to make changes after the quantity take-offs are finished, because revisions are so easy in a GIS.

Table of Land Use by Area

Future Land Use Designation	Total Acres	Built Acres	Vacant Acres	Constrained Acres	Vacant, Unconstrained Acres
Community Center Mixed Use	516	467	49	-	49
Corridor Business	1,306	749	555	44	511
Corridor Residential	648	418	230	25	205
Downtown	252	216	36	9	27
Employment	6,566	2,253	4,314	708	3,606
Government	4,788	1,541	3,246	494	2,753
Main Street Business	994	769	225	42	183
Neighborhood Mixed Use	382	305	77	7	70
Parks & Open Space	1,347	1	1,346	500	845
Residential Mixed Use	1,034	718	316	58	258
Rural	25,693	5,009	20,684	2,582	18,102
Rural Residential	3,328	2,614	714	65	649
Single Family Residential	21,657	12,368	9,289	1,464	7,825
Traditional Neighborhood	4,366	1,826	2,540	266	2,275
University District	1,520	878	641	53	588
Total	**74,393**	**30,132**	**44,261**	**6,316**	**37,944**

The GIS easily calculates the area of each land-use type.

Design guidelines

The comprehensive plan included a growth concept plan and a future land-use plan. The growth concept plan identifies specific improvement zones, each with its own design guidelines. Some of the improvement zones were transportation corridors: parkways, rural roads, commercial streets, boulevards, and main streets. The other proposals were development nodes including Downtown Athens, one regional center, seven community centers, and eight neighborhood centers.

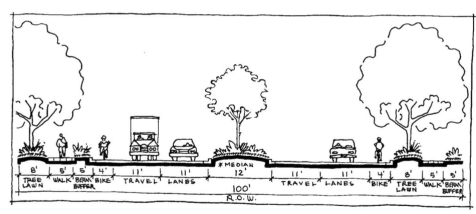

Design guidelines were developed for each of the corridors connecting the new urban centers.

Parcel by parcel

The other half of the GIS mapping for
Athens–Clark County is the future land-
use map. The proposed development centers and corridors caused zoning changes
for individual parcels, and these changes
became the Future Land Use Plan. This is
a very detailed recommendation of proposed zoning changes that will take several years to implement. By mapping the
new zoning densities, the GIS calculated
potential tax revenue under aggressive
and moderate growth scenarios.

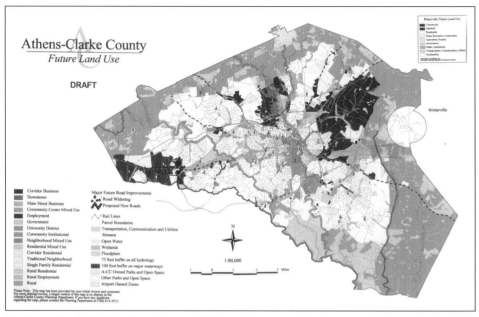

The Future Land Use Plan shows the potential for new homes, new businesses, and new tax revenues.

Icing on the cake

One of the most convincing images of any plan is a 3-D view. ArcView GIS can drape any map over a terrain model to make such a view. Various viewing angles and viewing can be simulated, as well as different sun angles.

The Athens–Clark County Comprehensive Plan puts the capabilities of GIS to the test in responding to the needs of large, diverse constituencies with complex issues in a short period of time. Fregonese Calthorpe Associates put the power of GIS to work by simulating future transportation systems, school systems, and environmental systems. Its comprehensive plan is balanced, flexible, and achievable. And the community, because it was involved from the start, supports the plan wholeheartedly.

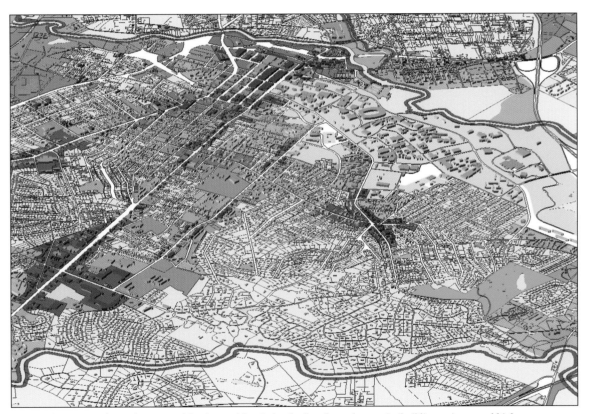

This bird's eye view shows the proposed land use with existing landmarks such as major buildings, rivers, and highways.

GAP ANALYSIS

One theme that is often unavailable in GIS data sets is vegetation. USGS quads, called digital line graphs (or DLGs) in their GIS format, will sometimes show forested areas or wood lots, but no designation of tree species. In areas with national forests you may be able to obtain timber yield maps, but vegetation maps meaningful to landscape architects are harder to find. If the site is small, field identification can be supplemented by maps drawn over aerial photos, then digitized. If an aerial photo of your site exists in your GIS, and if field survey data is available, the vegetation theme can be created digitally. If a state has completed its "GAP analysis," digital maps of vegetation will also be available.

Any project involving greenbelts, greenways, or natural corridors can benefit from a GAP analysis for that state. GAP is not an acronym: it's a program that identifies "gaps" in protected habitat for vertebrate species in the United States. The full name is National Biological Inventory Analysis Study. Administered by the National Biological Service, GAP is completed on a state-by-state basis as funding is provided by Congress.

The program began in Hawaii due to noticeable declines in bird species. The actual number of species included in the survey varies by state. In Arkansas, 457 terrestrial vertebrate species were studied. (Visit www.cast.uark.edu for details on Arkansas' GAP project.)

Each state develops its own procedure, but most follow a similar process.

Satellite imagery is obtained that covers the state. Each of these "scenes" must be purchased, and complete coverage can be costly.

The images are "interpreted" using any of a number of computer applications. The result is a vegetative cover map showing plant communities classified by their habitat potential for the designated wildlife species.

A map is then prepared for each animal species, showing its likely distribution. These are compared with field counts and other studies documenting known habitat.

An estimate is made of the overall population of each species and the type and amount of habitat necessary to sustain current numbers.

Finally, ownership is considered. Lands that already provide protection are identified, as well as those that are vulnerable to development or degradation, as from clear-cutting. The final report makes recommendations for target lands to be acquired or protected with easements.

Acknowledgments

Thanks to David Ausherman of Fregonese Calthorpe & Associates, Portland, Oregon.

Chapter 8

Save our river

EVEN BEFORE THEY HAD FINISHED the project in 1971, the Army Corps of Engineers had decided that channelization of the Kissimmee River, in central Florida, was not a good idea. In seven years, they had converted 103 miles of free-flowing river, interlaced with wetlands and teeming with wildlife, into 56 miles of straight, uniform channel. During the years that followed channelization, the South Florida Water Management District found that 90 percent of the waterfowl and 43,000 of 60,000 acres of floodplain had vanished. The district contacted the University of California at Berkeley, where scientists developed four restoration proposals that were tested in 1984 and 1985. One of these proposals is being used in restoring the river's entire length; this effort is still underway in 1999.

In the meantime, the area experienced some of the country's most rapid growth. Nearby Orlando saw the development of Disney World and a number of other theme parks, which greatly increased the number of tourists and tourism-related businesses. The local people adopted airboating, while retired snowbirds arrived with motorboats. The balance of nature in the Kissimmee watershed was upset in many ways.

In 1981, the Resources Rivers Act directed the district, and others, to provide recreation in "an environmentally acceptable manner." By 1990, the restoration area was already providing hiking, picnicking, fishing, boating, canoeing, and camping. When the Kissimmee River Restoration Act was passed in 1991, it set the stage for restoring the ecosystems, in addition to providing recreation. Shortly thereafter, a team of landscape architects, hydrology engineers, wildlife experts, vegetation specialists, and market analysts, led by E D S A \Edward D. Stone, Jr. and Associates, was hired to prepare a recreation management plan for the 56-mile river corridor that encompasses approximately 60,000 acres of land. Other restoration projects along the river were being implemented by other agencies.

The team took on the task of documenting the existing recreation facilities, studying population projections for the area, and estimating the future demand for various types of recreation. The team determined the number of people currently using the study area through permits issued for boating, fishing, and hunting, and from State Parks Department records. The team then developed environmental restoration proposals in areas removed from heavy recreation. Their primary objective was to produce a recreation and natural resources management plan that would not degrade the restored Kissimmee River ecosystem. Since the river is still not restored, the recreation effects had to be estimated against a future, healthy ecosystem.

Back to nature

The primary goals as stated by the Kissim-mee River Restoration Plan are:

1. To evaluate the ecological systems of the Kissimmee River and its surround-ings, and to determine their carrying capacity, or suitabilities for recre-ational development.

2. Using the determined suitabilities, to develop a recreation and management plan that enhances the natural and ecological integrity of the restored Kissimmee River system (Kissimmee River Inventory and Analysis Report, page 5.1).

The Kissimmee River Restoration Plan also lists three ecological goals:

1. Restore the natural fluctuation of water levels in the river and its associ-ated wetlands.

2. Provide conditions that are favorable to the natural restoration of vegetation and wildlife.

3. Use the natural energies of the river as much as possible.

Working with the system

The district had already been working in a GIS environment and had a great deal of data available in that format. E D S A elected to prepare its analyses in a GIS. Quoting from the report:

1. The analysis process should not be a study in preservation but an appli-cation of conservation, corresponding to a compromise between preserva-tionism and the recreational land de-velopment goals of the projects.

2. To determine the site's suitability for development, an overlay mapping process utilizing the Rules of Combi-nation would be used to examine the site's natural and man-made systems.

3. A Geographic Information System (GIS) would be developed to carry out the spatial analysis of the project area. The GIS would automate the overlay process and the combination of homogenous layers of information.

Assessing the land

Six components were studied, as listed below. A vulnerability model was pre-pared for each. The vulnerability rating assessed the degree to which recreation uses would affect each site characteristic. A few components also had quality mod-els prepared. The quality ratings mea-sured the potential of that characteristic to provide recreation use. In these examples, the quality model output was combined with the vulnerability model output to yield composite vulnerability maps. At the end, all six vulnerability maps were combined to form the Overall Composite Vulnerability Map. From this final map, restoration, recreation, and management recommendations were made.

Vegetation and soils characteristics

There are essentially four vegetation groups in the study area (upland forested and nonforested, and wetland forested and nonforested). With several subgroups, eighteen plant community or land cover categories were studied. Due to the hydric nature of the soils, and their strong link to the vegetation types, vegetation and soils were studied together. This work was directed by Milleson Environmental Consulting, which had done much of the field mapping in 1980.

Vulnerability of the vegetation and soils to human activity was determined by hydroperiod and groundwater, soils, fire, and physical disturbances. Values were assigned to each of the eighteen vegetation types for each of these four factors. The values for hydroperiod/groundwater were given twice the weight as the others, then all the values were summed. This is a classic McHargian overlay.

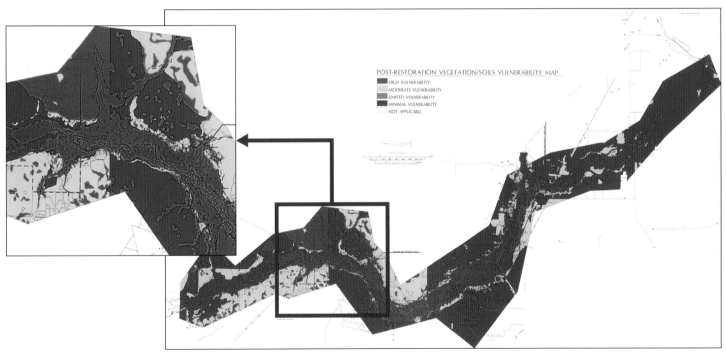

Post-Restoration Vegetation/Soils Vulnerability Map

Hydrologic and physiographic conditions

Five riparian zones were identified: channel, floodplain, transitional zones, tributary and water courses, and uplands. Hydrologic conditions were described by duration, velocity, stage-discharge relationships, stage-recession rates, and floodplain inundation frequencies. Physiographic conditions refer to the water conveyance, specifically the river channel, canal, and floodplain. Howard Searcy Consulting Engineers developed the model for hydrologic and physiographic conditions.

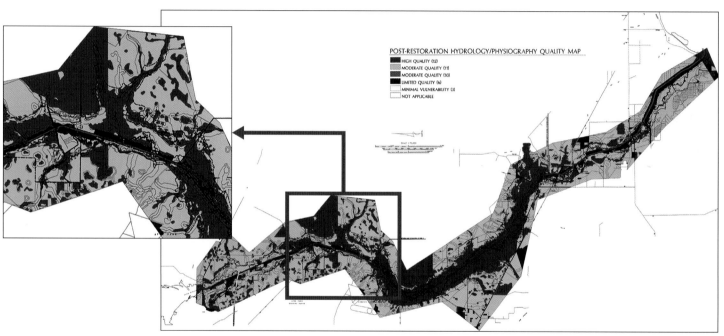

Post-Restoration Hydrology/Physiography Quality Map

Wildlife habitat

The Habitat Evaluation Procedures developed by the U.S. Fish and Wildlife Service in 1976 were used by the wildlife consultant, Breedlove, Dennis and Associates, Inc.

From a list of twenty-five indicator species, models were developed and run for eleven species. The standard for evaluation of habitat conditions is the Habitat Unit.

Habitat Units are determined by multiplying the acreage of specific habitat types by a measure of habitat quality called the Habitat Suitability Index (Kissimmee River Inventory and Analysis Report, page 5.47). Scores were derived for Florida water rats, bobcats, pig frogs, black crappie, common yellowthroat,

Florida ducks, ring-neck ducks, herons and egrets, field sparrows, and wild turkeys. Eight of these species live in wetlands and three species are associated with uplands. The maps for all eleven species were combined according to a set of rules to yield the Composite Habitat Suitability Map.

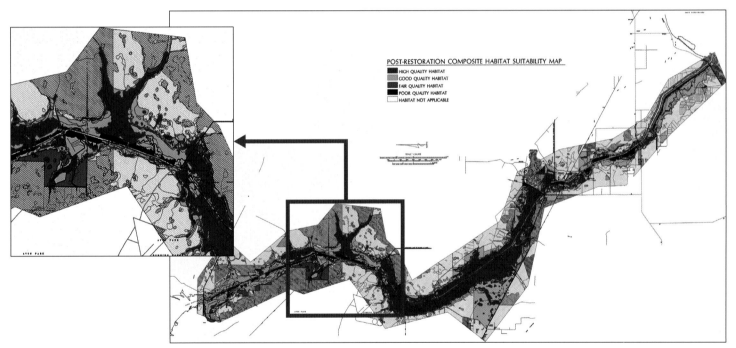

Post-Restoration Composite Habitat Suitability Map

Visual resources

E D S A adapted the Bureau of Land Management's Visual Resource Management System (VRM) to develop a model for assessing visual quality. This model used seven visual variables (landform, vegetation, water, color, adjacent scenery, scarcity, and cultural modifications). The model for visual absorption was based on six landscape variables (slope, soil stability and erosion potential, soil/vegetation contrast, vegetation regeneration potential, soil, and rock color contrast). A set of Visual Resources Rules of Combination were applied to the output of these two models in order to develop the Composite Visual Resources Vulnerability Map.

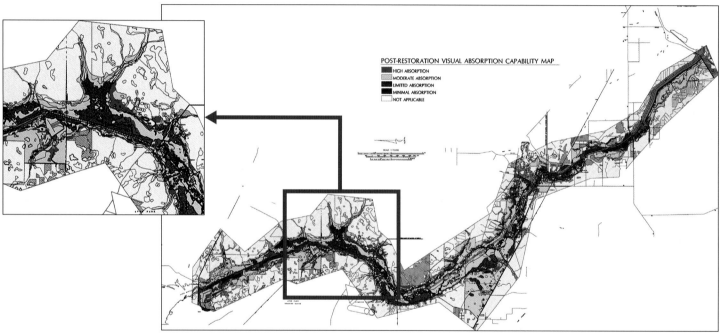

Post-Restoration Visual Absorption Capability Map

Historic and archaeological resources

The Florida Division of Historical Resources, Florida Site File, was the source of the information on twenty-nine historic sites within the study area. The immediate area of each site was defined as a circle 500 feet in diameter. Three additional concentric rings of 250 feet each were plotted by the GIS around each site. Moving from the center, each successive buffer zone had a lower vulnerability rating and a higher development potential.

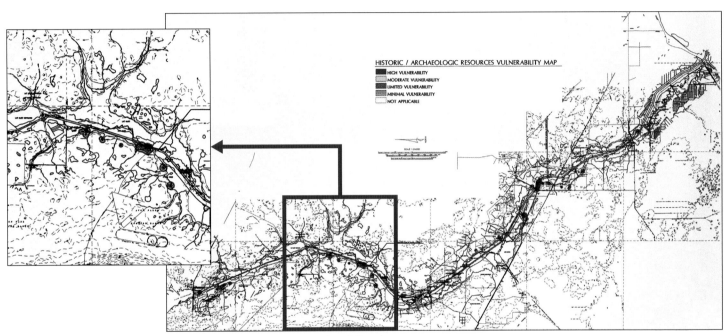

Historic/Archaeologic Resources Vulnerability Map

Recreation development potential/ownership

Five ownership categories were used to determine the recreation development potential. Lands already owned by the district present the fewest obstacles to immediate development and were rated highest. Three categories of ownership represent moderate recreation potential: those already slated for acquisition, state-owned lands, and federally owned lands. Some of the lands with the lowest recreation development potential are owned by the district, but with nonrecreation uses such as grazing, which will remain.

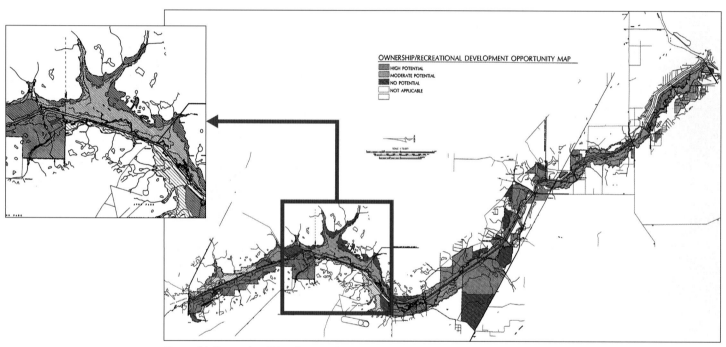

Ownership/Recreational Development Opportunity Map

The people's choice for land and water recreation

All six of the models were combined to form the Post-Restoration Composite Site Analysis/Development Suitability Map, shown below. Using input from an earlier citizens' design charette, another team member, Economics Research Associates (ERA), projected the recreation demand and studied the existing supply of recreation amenities. The supply and demand ratio was used to recommend total quantities for each of twenty-eight recreation types. By hand, E D S A then prepared three alternative solutions meeting these goals, which it presented to the District and the local community. The final compromise was developed manually into the Kissimmee River Conceptual Land Use and Natural Resource Guideline, also known as a "concept plan."

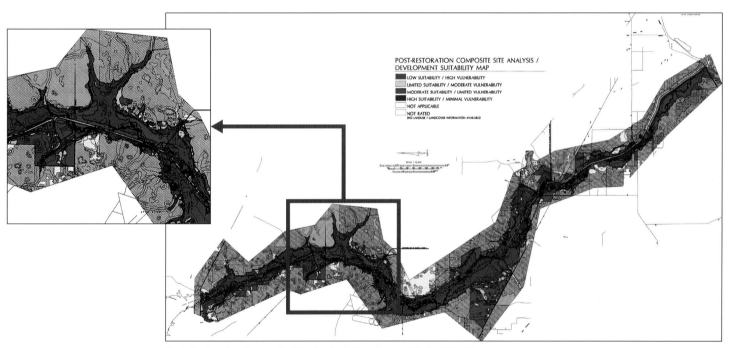

Post-Restoration Composite Site Analysis/Development Suitability Map

The hand-drawn maps

The real legacy of this sophisticated analysis is the "Land Use and Natural Resources Management Report." This document provides detailed information that will guide the district in its daily operations and in developing each successive project. The legitimacy of the recreation proposals comes from the vulnerability and quality models, which were designed to protect the evolving river system.

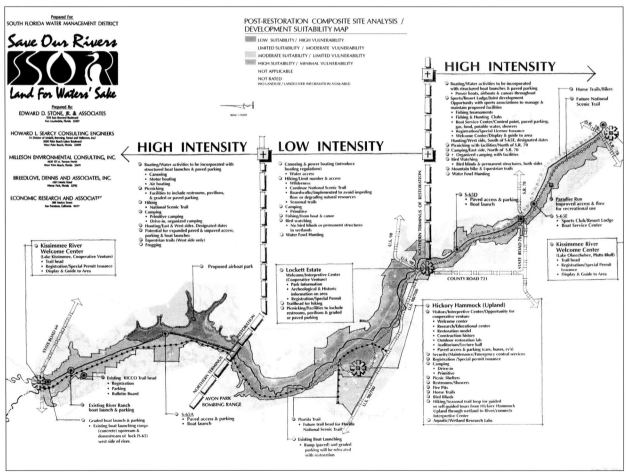

Conceptual Landuse and Natural Resource Guideline

Conclusion

The Kissimmee Save Our River project is an in-depth suitability mapping exercise. Information was gathered from many sources and evaluated by designers, scientists, engineers, and market analysts. The mathematical and geographic operators of ArcInfo were employed, following the rules of each model, to produce the six vulnerability maps.

The GIS was ideal for fine-tuning the value assignments. If the client or other interested parties had comments to make, slight or large value adjustments could be made quickly and easily. Adjustments can be made in the model as well as to the graphics. In the Kissimmee River project, E D S A converted the digital maps into hand-drawn maps and added features and notes to the final site plan.

What is unique about the Kissimmee River restoration is that the base conditions did not yet exist. At the time of the study, the channel had not been removed and the historic riverbed had not yet been restored. The vegetation had not yet regenerated itself, although studies showed that natural regeneration was likely. The GIS allowed the team to study a future, restored floodplain.

Finally, because the data is in digital form, and the models and GIS operators are very well documented, the district can continue to update the suitability maps into the future. As recreation demands change, or as the site regenerates itself, perhaps in unanticipated ways, the models can be rerun to keep the plan current and responsive.

Acknowledgments

Thanks to the following:

Paul Kissinger of Edward D. Stone, Jr. and Associates, Fort Lauderdale, Florida

Fred Davis, Director, Land Stewardship Division, and Lee Henderson, Project Manager, both of South Florida Water Management District

••••••

Chapter 9

Gold in the water

THE SAN FRANCISCO BAY AREA WATER SUPPLY SYSTEM was built with great foresight and ambition. Although San Francisco had been settled for seventy years, the city was not incorporated until 1850, when the discovery of gold brought thousands to California. The Spring Valley Water Works, one of the predecessors to today's San Francisco Public Utilities Commission (SFPUC), initiated a water system for the city in 1860. It also began acquiring land on the peninsula south of San Francisco and in 1864 completed the dam for the first of five reservoirs to be built in this watershed.

In 1875, the Spring Valley Water Company began purchasing land and building dams across the bay, in the Alameda watershed. However, the city fathers could see that even these additional reservoirs would not supply enough water for the kind of population growth they had in mind.

Representatives of the City of San Francisco went to the U.S. Congress and in 1913 received permission to build an impoundment and power-generating reservoir in the Sierra Nevada. The construction of the Hetch Hetchy Reservoir was controversial, even in the early years of this century, because it flooded one of the most beautiful canyons in Yosemite National Park. The headwaters of the Tuolumne River are more than 150 miles from San Francisco, but water from the Hetch Hetchy Reservoir was transported via aqueduct to the Crystal Springs Reservoir, on the peninsula, in October of 1934. Over the years, five more reservoirs in the Sierra Nevada have been built and linked to the system of tunnels, pipes, and power-generating plants that conduct the water to the Alameda and Peninsula reservoirs.

The system now delivers 300,000 gallons per day to Bay Area users.

The entire water supply of the greater Bay Area passes through the impoundments of the Peninsula and Alameda watersheds. While the Peninsula watershed does not produce that much water, these lakes are the last holding reservoirs before treatment and delivery of the Hetch Hetchy supplies. Two million residents rely on the health of these watersheds to protect the quality and dependability of their water.

Reservoirs in the Sierra Nevada are the source of most of California's water.

A fragile watershed

The Peninsula watershed covers 23,000 acres of nearly pristine lands. Interstate 280 runs along the ridgeline, which forms the eastern boundary of the watershed. The area east of the ridge is crowded by eight suburban cities extending from San Bruno to Redwood City. The western edge of the watershed is the crest of Montara Mountain, and several intermediate ridges divide the combined watershed.

The three primary threats are fire, erosion, and pollution.

Since there has been no major fire in the last century, the accumulated fuel loads are quite sizable and a large fire would be devastating. Fire could also trigger widespread erosion and greatly diminish the visual quality of the area.

Should the land cover be lost, due to fire, pest, or disease, subsequent erosion would result in loss of soil needed to promote future plant growth. Soil erosion would cause turbidity of the water and sedimentation, leading to a serious reduction in the holding capacity of each impoundment. Earthquakes can also trigger landslides and subsequent erosion. The San Andreas Fault runs through the three major reservoirs on the peninsula and other major faults traverse the watershed.

Pesticides and fertilizers from farms and the golf course, gas and oil spills from vehicles, runoff from roads, and dumping of jet fuel from approaching aircraft are among the hazardous materials threatening the water supply. Wildlife is also known to introduce pathogens.

The greatest protection is afforded by the SFPUC's ownership of most of the watershed. There are three small inholdings, totaling 1,200 acres, but these are well managed and pose little risk to the watershed. There are several overlay districts including the San Francisco State Peninsula Fish and Game Refuge, a scenic easement, and a scenic and recreation easement. The political mechanisms are in place to protect the watershed; the threats come from natural events or the actions of people.

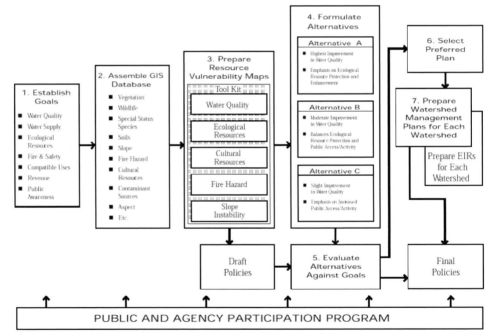

EDAW developed the process above and completed the project using ArcInfo. Simultaneously, plans for the Alameda watersheds were underway.

Protect water quality above all else

In 1992, SFPUC decided to update its watershed management plan, and a team headed by EDAW's San Francisco office was selected. To establish goals for the project, the team worked with a group of SFPUC staff called the Watershed Planning Committee. The team also met with the local communities at three points in the process: to establish goals, and to review interim and then final results. The primary goal, agreed to by all stakeholders, was:

Maintain and improve source water quality to protect public health and safety.

The following six secondary goals were also identified:

1. Maximize the contribution of the watersheds to the water supply.

2. Preserve and enhance the ecological and cultural resources of the watersheds.

3. Protect the watershed, adjacent urban areas, and the public from fire and other hazards.

4. Continue existing compatible uses and provide opportunities for additional compatible uses on watershed lands including educational, recreational, and scientific uses.

5. Provide a balance between financial resources, revenue generation activities, and overall benefits.

6. Enhance public awareness of water quality, water supply, conservation, and watershed protection activities.

Using the goals as directives, EDAW's design team assembled basic GIS data and designed a process for evaluating the watershed. The basic data types included geology and soils, elevation, hydrology, vegetation, rare or endangered plants and animals, habitats (field recorded and potential), fisheries, archaeologic and historic features, land status (ownership, leases, and overlay districts), roads, trails, utilities, and recreation facilities.

Some of the basic data types were acted on by GIS operators to derive new maps. Examples of derived maps are slope (derived from elevation), vegetation fuel loads (derived from vegetation communities), and dwelling density (derived from land status).

Along with the basic data, the derived maps formed the building blocks of models to create vulnerability maps. A model is the set of step-by-step instructions given the computer to combine data in mathematic manipulations or graphic overlays. EDAW developed models to generate five vulnerability maps for ecological resources, fire hazard, slope instability, cultural resources, and water quality.

Ecology model tells tale of sensitivity

Environmental Science Associates (ESA)
and their ecology specialist, Diane Renshaw, provided the data and classification
systems for the vegetation and wildlife
studies. ESA developed the model for the
Composite Ecological Sensitivity Zones,
which combined the findings of the sensitive vegetation and wildlife communities,
and maps of special-status species (rare or
endangered plants and animals).

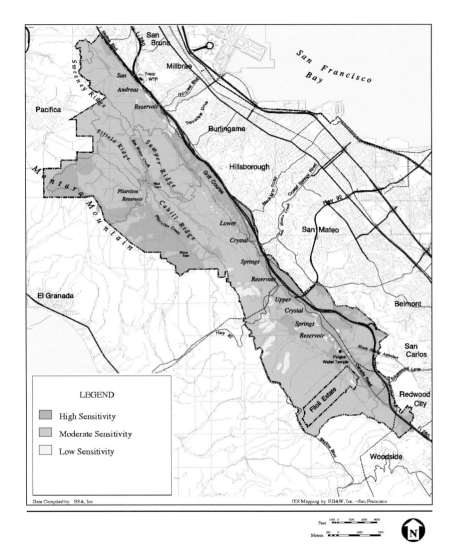

LEGEND

High Sensitivity

Moderate Sensitivity

Low Sensitivity

Data Compiled by ESA, Inc.   GIS Mapping by EDAW, Inc. –San Francisco

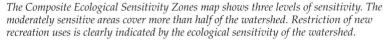

The Composite Ecological Sensitivity Zones map shows three levels of sensitivity. The
moderately sensitive areas cover more than half of the watershed. Restriction of new
recreation uses is clearly indicated by the ecological sensitivity of the watershed.

Frightening fire hazard

Fire hazard is revealed by combining data from the vegetation fuel loads, slope, and dwelling densities maps. The fire hazard data was compiled by ESA, while the fire hazard model was developed by Wildland Resource Management (WRM). WRM followed guidelines set out by the California State Assembly's Bates Bill, which was passed in response to the disastrous fires in Oakland. A fire management plan was prepared after the watershed study based on fire simulation models shown here.

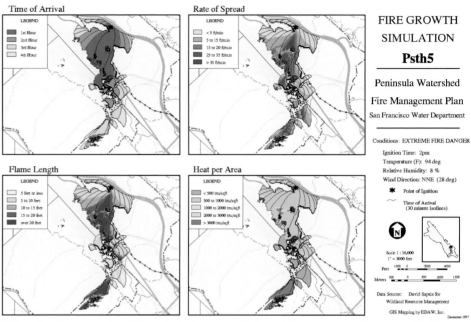

This series of maps convinced the watershed managers that vegetation management was a worthwhile investment. About 33 percent of the watershed has high fire potential.

Slope instability

By combining the raw data for soils with
the slope maps, then selecting from those
resultant soil/slope categories the ones
that are rated for severe and very severe
erosion potential, the analysts were able to
determine slope instability. Maps showing
historic landslide sites were then added
for predicted landslide potential. The Natural Resources Conservation Service (for-
merly the Soil Conservation Service) is
converting most of its soils maps and ratings into GIS format, which will be available for many counties over the Internet.

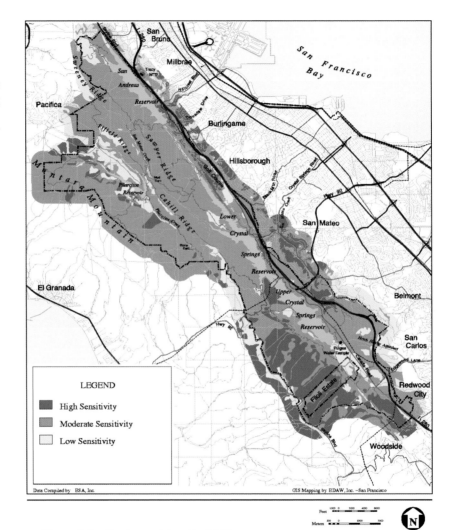

Figure 2-2   Erosion and Land Instability

Land instability ratings showed 20 percent high and about 70 percent moderate.

Cultural sensitivity survey reveals history

David Chavez and Associates provided
the base data for historic structures and
prehistoric archaeological sites. Historic
features included early water conveyances
and an old stage road. The map of cultural
sensitivity zones resulted from a compara-
tive ranking of the historical resources.
The archaeological basemaps were not
released to the public.

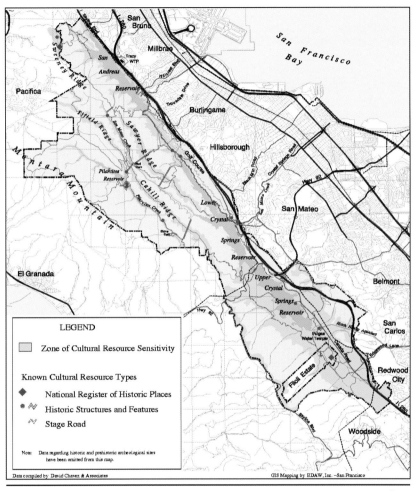

Figure 2-8 **Known Cultural Resources and
Potential Sensitivity Zones**

Original Scale 1 : 24,000

*The composite map shows that the greatest sensitivity for cultural resources lies in the
southeastern quarter of the watershed.*

Water quality model

The ratio of imported water to local runoff dictates the water quality as much as surface conditions in the immediate watershed. The model for water quality was based on a combination of approaches from similar studies throughout the United States. Factors included the size of the contributing watershed and its rainfall intensity, and characteristics of soils, vegetative cover, and wildlife concentrations.

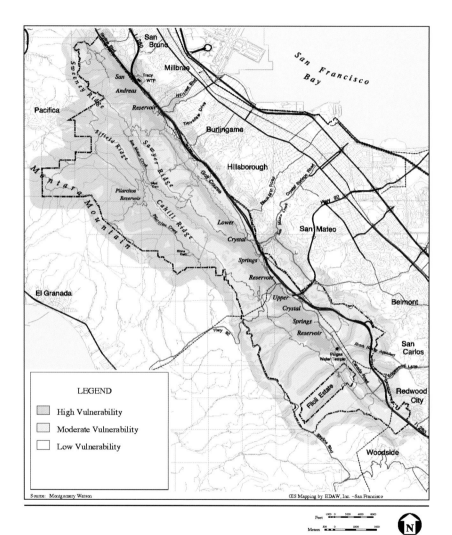

Figure 2-3 Composite Water Quality Vulnerability Zones   Original Scale 1 : 24,000

Over half (60 percent) of the watershed has high vulnerability for water quality.

Prior to site design

The high sensitivity areas of four out of the five vulnerability maps were extracted and superimposed on a single map to form the "Composite High Sensitivity Zones" map. The cultural sensitivity map was not included because policies were already in place to protect cultural resources.

This map shows that about 10 percent of the watershed has no conditions that receive a "high sensitivity rating," and about 35 percent has two or more conditions with "high sensitivity ratings." It is not only the proportion of high sensitivity ratings that directed formulation of the management policies, but their physical relationship to one another and to features such as roads and reservoirs. Ease of access, nearness to homes and businesses, and visibility from the freeway all played a role in developing management policies.

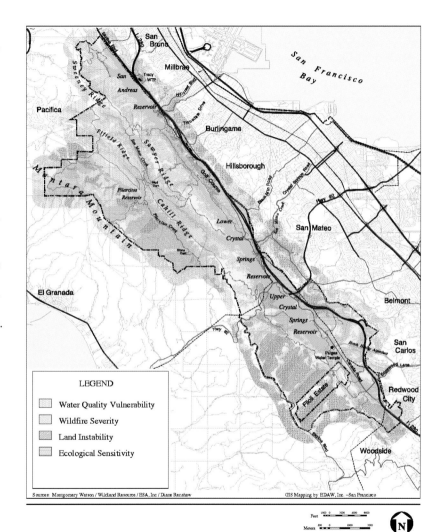

LEGEND

Water Quality Vulnerability

Wildfire Severity

Land Instability

Ecological Sensitivity

Sources: Montgomery Watson / Wildland Resource / BSA, Inc / Diane Renshaw   GIS Mapping by EDAW, Inc. –San Francisco

Figure 2-1   Composite High Sensitivity Zones   Original Scale 1 : 24,000

The distribution of high sensitivity zones guided the design team as it proposed locations for new recreation amenities and developed management strategies. There is pressure to provide more recreation than initially proposed, which will result in more mitigation measures.

Design of new site amenities

Because so much of the watershed is extremely sensitive to development, the proposals for physical improvements are rather limited. A new golf course in the less sensitive southeast corner of the watershed is proposed, in addition to retention of an existing golf course across I-280 from Hillsborough. These leases will generate revenue for the SFPUC to offset management costs of the watershed.

In addition to the golf course, there are four proposals for expansion of the trail system. The proposals vary in their alignment, access, and use. The chosen proposal will allow for unrestricted access by hikers, equestrians, and bicyclists, with annual reviews to determine whether the latter two groups will be allowed to continue. The chart summarizes each proposal's fulfillment of the established goals. The evaluations in the chart were based on the composite sensitivity map and its four component maps.

		Existing	No Action	Alternative A	Alternative B	Alternative C	Preferred Plan
PRIMARY GOAL	Maintain and Improve Source Water Quality to Protect Public Health and Safety	○	○	●	◐	◐	●
SECONDARY GOALS	Maximize the Contribution of the Watersheds to Water Supply.	◐	●	●	◐	●	●
	Preserve and Enhance the Ecological and Cultural Resources of the Watersheds.	○	○	●	●	○	●
	Protect the Watersheds, Adjacent Urban Areas, and the Public from Fire and Other Hazards.	○	◐	●	●	◐	●
	Continue Existing Compatible Uses and Provide Opportunities for Potential Compatible Uses on Watershed Lands including Educational, Recreational and Scientific.	○	○	◐	●	●	●
	Provide a Balance between Financial Resources, Revenue Generation Activities and Overall Benefits.	◐	○	◐	◐	◐	◐
	Enhance Public Awareness of Water Quality, Water Supply, Conservation, and Watershed Protection Activities.	○	○	●	●	◐	●

● Alternative is Highly Responsive to the Goal.   ◐ Alternative is Moderately Responsive to the Goal.   ○ Alternative has a Low Response to the Goal.

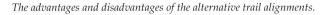

The advantages and disadvantages of the alternative trail alignments.

GIS in action

By far, the major use of the GIS products is in the development of management policies. Much of the Peninsula Watershed Management Plan is devoted to detailed lists of policies relating to the one primary and six secondary goals. To make them easier for the SFPUC staff to use, these policy recommendations are expanded and reorganized into twenty-two action topics and subtopics. Many of the recommendations refer to monitoring techniques, which are tied in turn to ongoing mapping in a GIS and future updating of the vulnerability maps.

GIS is a logical tool for watershed monitoring and management. Watersheds are dynamic in nature, directly affected by their upstream uses and affecting their downstream uses. Runoff and its attendant effects are exponentially increased as hard surfacing continues. New grading, paving, construction, and land-use changes make watersheds anything but static environments. With advances in photoimaging, records of fires are much more easily added to the equation. With GIS assistance, watershed managers can be more effective guardians, and design professionals can be more effective advisors, than ever before.

Acknowledgments

Thanks to David Blau and Peter Jonas of EDAW, Inc., San Francisco, California.

Chapter 10

Little League on the Tennessee River

CHATTANOOGA, TENNESSEE, IS A PICTURESQUE CITY along the Tennessee River, near the Georgia state line. North of the city, the river is dammed to form Chickamauga Lake, a source of recreation and beauty for city residents. Founded on historic water, rail, and highway shipping routes, many of the city's 150,000 inhabitants are employed in manufacturing. Recent urban redevelopment efforts have been nationally recognized and Chattanooga is planning for new growth well into the next century.

In 1998, Chattanooga's Department of Parks and Recreation (DPR) undertook a ten-year update of its recreation master plan, locally known as RECREATE 2008! They chose the Philadelphia office of Wallace Roberts & Todd (WRT) to prepare the plan. WRT conducted the public input sessions, inventoried existing recreation facilities, identified recreation demand and deficiencies, developed fiscal and management recommendations, and prepared the final citywide master plan. The firm did this in only eight months with the help of ArcView GIS software.

Electronic CADD files were provided by the Regional Planning Agency, which WRT converted into ArcView GIS coverages to form a basemap of the city. In the next few months, WRT obtained parcel-level information about every public park and recreational facility within Chattanooga and created ArcView GIS maps and corresponding databases describing acreage, ownership, and specific facilities (e.g., baseball fields, tennis courts). This inventory was used to determine the shortages of different recreation amenities throughout the city.

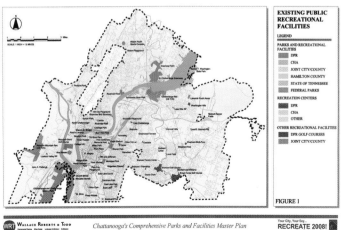

FIGURE 1

WRT used census data to map population densities and ages. Recreation facilities (shown here) are provided by many agencies.

WALLACE ROBERTS & TODD   *Chattanooga's Comprehensive Parks and Facilities Master Plan*   RECREATE 2008!

Recreation standards

After World War II, recreation was recognized as playing an important role in American lives, and this led to the establishment of recreation standards. The National Recreation and Parks Association (NRPA) publishes standards representing the number of facilities required per person, with regional variations. WRT compared the supply of existing recreation facilities in Chattanooga against the NRPA's recommendations and standards set by Memphis, Tennessee; Knoxville, Tennessee; and Louisville, Kentucky. These studies helped WRT understand how Chattanooga's provision of recreational facilities compared with other major southern cities.

Concurrent with developing the recreational needs of the city, WRT conducted an intensive public participation program. Sixteen community meetings were held initially, and WRT recorded the comments from all those meetings in its final report. Many residents were concerned with the lack of maintenance of facilities, rather than a lack of facilities. This was especially true of recreation centers: these buildings traditionally have high levels of year-round use.

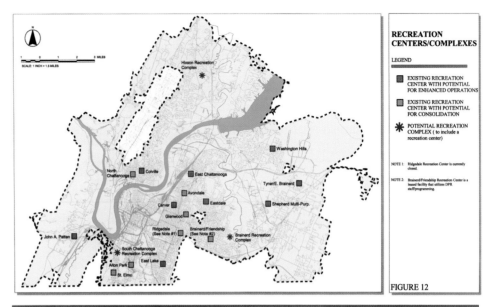

Recreation centers provide year-round activities for many age groups.

Population patterns

Next, WRT used U.S. census data to plot population densities in the various communities throughout Chattanooga. This exercise was followed with maps showing age distribution: under 5 years of age, 5 to 19 years, 20 to 64 years, and 65 and over. From the 1990 census data, WRT learned that the highest population density was in three census tracts in the downtown area. They found that the greatest number of children (5 to 19 years old) were in the southern and middle portion of the city and in East Brainerd. Most seniors were concentrated in the urban core. These maps helped refine the plan's recommendations so the right type of recreation facilities would be located near the appropriate age group.

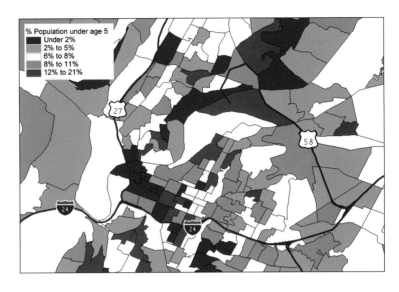

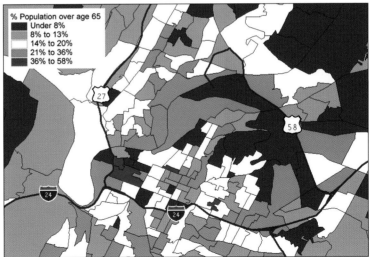

Census data makes it easy to locate the neighborhoods with larger numbers of seniors and those areas with the most children.

Demand minus supply

The census data comes in two parts, tables and maps. The smallest unit for aggregating data is the census tract, and in many cases the tracts are coincident with neighborhoods. The standards set by NRPA were used to calculate recreation demand for each neighborhood. When compared with the recreation demand, an inventory of existing facilities may demonstrate satisfactory use, overuse, or underuse. Twelve uses were evaluated.

The design team found that the number of baseball fields provided by the city exceeded the NRPA's recommended standards. The city's provision of golf courses and tennis courts were close to the NRPA standards, and the number of soccer fields, outdoor basketball courts, football fields, and pools, fell well below established standards. The NRPA does not list standards for recreation centers, playgrounds, or open play areas, but these needs had been established in the public meetings.

Mapping the needs

Neighborhood parks were mapped surrounded by a 1-mile radius, representing a realistic service area, unless interrupted by significant physical barriers such as rivers or freeways. These service area maps readily identified areas of the city that did not have enough neighborhood parks. WRT presented these findings in three community workshops and another public meeting. Throughout the process, the team worked closely with DPR staff, the Citizen's Task Force, the Regional Planning Agency, and members of the city council, to make sure their conclusions were accurate.

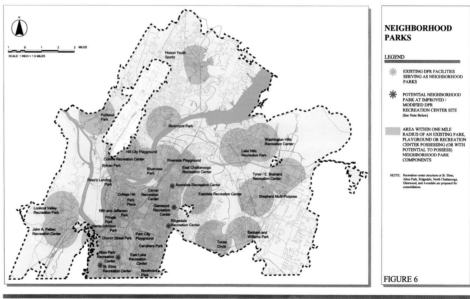

The white and light green areas of the city map are not served by existing neighborhood parks.

Satisfying the needs

With the needs assessment complete, it became clear that Chattanooga was in need of parks and recreation centers that were closer to their users and had higher quality facilities. To satisfy these needs, WRT recommended that DPR consolidate or close some of its facilities and improve others. WRT also proposed adding facilities, but mostly at existing school sites, in order to save land acquisition costs. This strategy was reflected on a GIS map that showed how park facilities at school sites would help fill gaps in neighborhood park service. The "DPR Facility Plan Concept: 2008" is the map of the proposed master plan found in the report, RECREATE 2008! The report also includes text describing specific recommendations for facilities and programs.

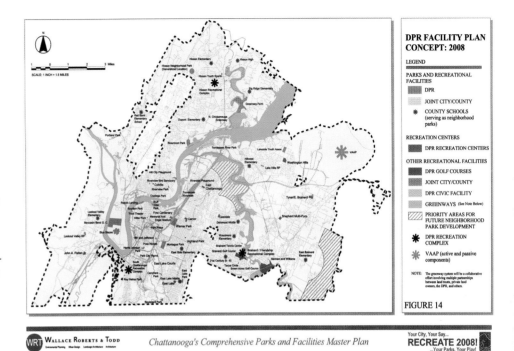

This map proposes the ultimate build-out of Chattanooga's park and recreation system, showing the retention of some existing facilities, creation of new ones, and identification of areas designated for parkland acquisition.

No sitting on the shelf for this plan

The total cost of implementing the recommendations of the master plan was estimated at $65 million. Priorities were expressed as Phase One (first three years), Phase Two (years four, five, and six), and Phase Three (years seven through ten). Increased operating and maintenance costs were also calculated to cover newly acquired or expanded parks. GIS files coupled with GIS measurement functions provided valuable assistance in calculating capital improvements and estimating the costs of operating and maintaining the parks.

WRT's design team then pursued a thorough examination of potential funding mechanisms for implementing the master plan. These options included special tax revenues, special assessment districts, a parks and open space district, parkland dedication in lieu of fees, open space/cluster subdivisions, a wetland mitigation bank, a conservation easement program, and several more. All the GIS maps and tables generated for the master plan have been forwarded to the Parks and Recreation Department in digital format and will be updated as it implements portions of the master plan.

The DPR will continue to use the master plan files to update annual budgets and shape its capital improvement plans.

Capital cost estimates

Category	Top priority	Second priority	Third priority
Parkland acquisition	$ 820,000	$ 150,000	$ 200,000
Existing park upgrades	$ 4,687,000	$ 3,352,000	$ 7,358,000
Existing recreation center improvements	$ 3,750,000	$ 1,500,000	$ 1,500,000
New park improvements	$ 13,645,000	$ 9,990,000	$ 890,000
Miscellaneous new facilities	$ 5,030,000	$ 1,225,000	$ 120,000
Consolidations	$ 210,000	$ 135,000	$ —
Planning studies	$ 130,000	$ —	$ —
Subtotal	**$ 28,272,000**	**$ 16,352,000**	**$ 10,068,000**
20% contingency	$ 5,654,400	$ 3,270,400	$ 2,013,600
Total (rounded)	**$ 33,926,000**	**$ 19,622,000**	**$ 12,082,000**
Total cumulative costs	**$ 33,926,000**	**$ 53,548,000**	**$ 65,630,000**

Implementation of new facilities inherently means an increased maintenance budget.

Designers and societal needs

This study used the census files to develop recreation needs throughout Chattanooga and to fine-tune its neighborhood recommendations. Social services from health departments to housing authorities to real estate brokers are tapping into digital databases to help them make decisions. The design professions have traditionally neglected statistical research in favor of public input. In addition to workshop facilitators, database experts may soon be a part of the landscape architect's design team.

Acknowledgments

Thanks to Bill Hartman of Wallace, Roberts & Todd, Philadelphia, Pennsylvania.

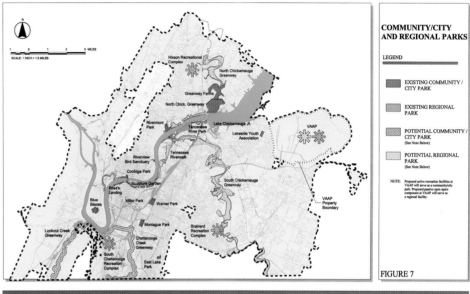

The various recreation providers can use the GIS files to coordinate their implementation efforts.

Chapter 11

Who needs another method?

AS GENERALISTS, LANDSCAPE ARCHITECTS HAVE AN IMPORTANT ROLE TO PLAY on interdisciplinary design teams. It is landscape architects who often act as liaisons to bring the scientists and the designers together. The digital revolution has made changes in the hard sciences, the social sciences, municipal government, and the design world. Geographic information systems are being used by everyone—real estate agents, city planners, census takers, 911 emergency aid providers, and on and on. While engineers, biologists, and planners have taken GIS seriously, most landscape architects have not. As a result, they have been left out of many exciting projects. GIS is a tool that connects databases to maps. As mapmakers, landscape architects need to be using GIS.

The GIS Graphic Method was developed by the author to make GIS more comfortable for landscape architects. The method follows the landscape architect's design process by applying familiar actions to GIS data and producing site designs.

Landscape architects voice several complaints about GIS. They say the data is not accurate enough or at a small enough resolution for real design work. They say that learning to use GIS is impossible for those who did not grow up with computers. They say that the computer is too rigid and they can only design using the fluid strokes of pencils on paper. None of these complaints is valid, as we will see.

CAD drawings can be extremely precise. With increasing ease, GIS accepts CAD drawings and brings that level of detail to the database. With similar ease, GIS drawings can be imported into CAD for preparation of construction documents and estimates.

GIS programs have become quite user-friendly. ArcView GIS is one of the easiest to learn, with many graphic interfaces and logical procedures. You can even have someone else do the actual computer work for you. Many principals work closely with GIS experts who are either on staff or subconsultants.

Design is a fluid exercise, connecting the right sides of our brains with our hands as we visualize the built environment. The GIS Graphic Method does not surrender this process to automation—the design is still done manually—but it allows landscape architects to work with existing digital data, to interact with other design professionals, and to provide results in a format preferred by many clients.

On the same page

For the benefit of this discussion, the specific design process on which the GIS Graphic Method is based will be documented below. Those landscape architects who have been preparing site plans for many years may not consciously follow a process. For them the process has become subconscious. However, we need a blueprint to follow so we can see how each step is accomplished with GIS. This process is certainly not the only one, but it is the one that the GIS Graphic Method follows.

In this process, seven steps lead one to a preliminary design. The preliminary design is then refined through design tests, design approval, further revisions, and construction documents. The preparatory steps include:

1. Site inventory

2. Program research

3. Concept initiation

4. Site analysis

5. Spatial diagrams

6. Active zone plan

7. Preliminary site design

The finishing steps include design tests, revised preliminary site design, client or agency approvals, design development, construction documents (PS&E), bidding, observation, and postconstruction review.

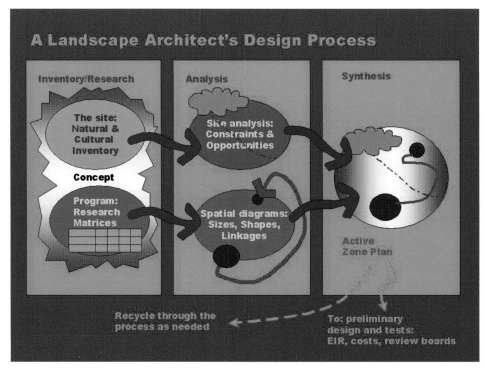

One version of the design process. The diagram shown covers the preparatory steps under the general headings of Inventory/Research (steps 1, 2, and 3), Analysis (steps 4 and 5), and Synthesis (steps 6 and 7).

Overview

This process begins by considering the dual entities of site and program. The site inventory is the collection of natural and cultural information about the site. This information may come from the client, the civil engineer, the county clerk's office, such experts as biologists or hydrologists, site managers, photos, archives, online data warehouses, interviews, and many other sources.

The program is the list of proposed uses and its research includes one's own experience, library and Internet research, client preferences, market analysis, public meetings, interviews, and preference surveys. The results of program research may be summarized in matrices. One matrix may relate ideal site conditions to each of the proposed uses; another might summarize minimum and maximum sizes of facilities, or the ages of each user group; another may rank the preferences of the community for each activity; still another may show relative costs of the various facilities. The matrices should include all the factors that are important to this project: the client's wishes, goals, and objectives; the relevant ordinances; the results of studies by outside experts.

There is probably more debate about the meaning of concept in design than there is about any other issue. In this discussion, concept will be a broad term with several meanings. The spatial diagrams may have a concept describing the layout, such as nested, satellite, or hierarchical. The active zone plan may have a concept that describes the way the facilities have been placed on the site, such as environmentally sensitive, or secretive. The preliminary design may have a concept that describes the forms and materials, such as Mediterranean, or rustic. Allegorical concepts are widely used in site design and detail design. The concept originates in the site inventory and program research, and may manifest itself at several points in the design process.

Proceeding to the analysis, we prepare the site analysis and spatial diagrams. The site analysis shows only those conditions that are relevant to the decisions being made. If every type of information were shown over the entire site, the site analysis would be unreadable. So, as an example, the areas that are too steep for building are shown, but not all the slope categories. The utilities easement may be shown, but not the boundary of the school district, which bisects the site. Only the tree canopy may be shown, and not the grasslands. On another project, the grasslands and tree canopy may be shown, and not the disturbed areas. The individual theme maps, such as vegetation or all the categories of slope, will be available to the designer, but the site analysis is the combined map of the critical site information, not all the site information.

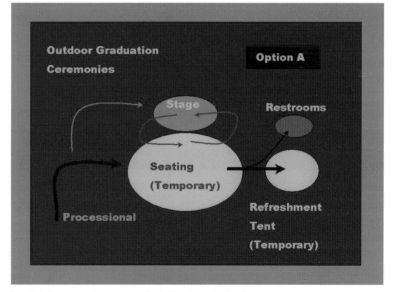

Spatial diagrams show physical relationships in the abstract.

The spatial diagrams show the relationship of one use to another. Often called "bubble diagrams," this series of layouts shows the relative sizes of each activity zone, their physical proximity to one another, what linkages are desirable, and if visual or physical barriers are necessary. Linkage types may include vehicular circulation, pedestrian routes, service routes, and so on. The bubble diagrams should not anticipate site conditions: the diagrams should examine these relationships in the abstract. Dozens of spatial diagrams may be generated, from which the designer will select the best three or four.

The model

The active zone plan fits one spatial diagram at a time onto the site analysis. In this step, each spatial diagram is positioned on the site following the rules established in the program matrices. Three or four valid active zone plans may result and each may be carried through preliminary design and testing. The active zone plan still shows "bubbles" (representing the use zones or facilities) and "arrows" (for circulation routes). It is often advantageous to take the active zone plan to public and client meetings, as it requires the participants to talk about major site issues, before considering design implementation issues.

The preliminary design gives form to the active zone plan. This step changes "bubbles" into pavements, lawns, or planting beds, and "arrows" into driveways and sidewalks. In the preliminary design, what was shown as a focal point on the active zone plan may become a water feature or a piece of sculpture.

Design tests include environmental review, cost estimates, client review, community presentations, design review board oversight, ordinance compliance, or other performance criteria. These tests can be greatly expedited with a GIS by using the measuring and reporting tools.

The entire process or parts of it may be repeated as objectives change or new information is received. After the client or a review board approves the design, major changes are avoided, but minor revisions continue throughout the process. Design development gives substance to the preliminary design. Construction details are designed for all components; earth forms and planting palettes are developed. The design process requires that we make all the decisions necessary for successful implementation of the project.

Same process, new format

The very same steps can be followed when the format is GIS. The same types of natural and cultural information will need to be collected, although in digital form. The process begins with fact finding about the site and researching the program of uses. Design concepts are developed from insights about the property, the client's goals, or an interesting bit of program research.

The difference in a GIS is that maps are created electronically. So, when selecting the vegetation types or soil types that are critical for design decisions, the designer must isolate the important data from the not-so-important data. Various GIS tools are used to meet this objective, but the goal is the same: assemble the critical data from which you will create a site analysis.

At one time, even as recently as the early part of this decade, collecting digital data was an overwhelming task. Data sets had to be built from scratch, using highly skilled GIS technicians. Major initiatives by federal, state, and local planners have made enormous amounts of data available. Advances in software have dramatically reduced the time it takes to learn GIS functions, from creating data to generating maps.

Program research is exactly the same in a GIS as it is in a manual project. Good sources of information about the activities are consulted and summarized in matrices. Your professional experience is a source of information.

An advantage of using GIS files is that measurements can be generated very quickly. If you need to know how much of a certain site condition exists, simply ask. The report functions in ArcView GIS can be used to note the amount of an existing condition, either as raw acreage or as its proportion of the total acreage. Calculation of area, length, or perimeter of each site condition can be quite handy when filling the records in matrices. Another advantage of GIS is that existing databases, such as census files, can provide demographic data that is automatically correlated to geographic areas.

Concept formulation does not vary from the manual method. Ideas coalesce from clues in the site's characteristics and our program research. Concepts will materialize whether the site data is in digital or paper format. We must not allow the technology to distract us from our creativity. The process is the same, the differences, small—work products exist in cyberspace, not on tracing paper.

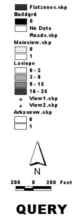

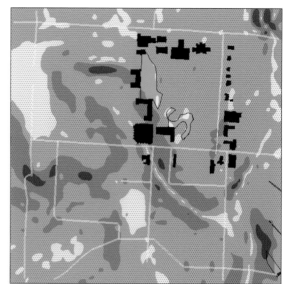

QUERY BUILDER

with flat zones selected
(in yellow)

Use the Query Builder in ArcView GIS to select a particular condition to show in the site analysis. In this example, the flat areas (0 to 2 percent) have been selected from all slope types.

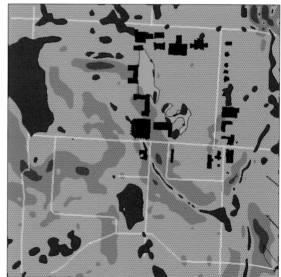

QUERY BUILDER

Flatzones become a separate theme
(in purple)

When the flat areas are selected they display in yellow. When they have become a separate theme another color may be chosen, such as purple, shown here. Selection of specific attributes is important when assembling a legible site analysis.

GIS Graphic Method is not suitability mapping

The site analysis is the key to this digital process. There is a significant difference between the GIS Graphic Method and suitability mapping or the McHarg overlay method. The McHarg method assigns values to site conditions based on the suitability of that condition for the use being considered (McHarg, 1997). For instance, if a highway corridor is being routed, each soil type will be assigned a suitability rating for its ability to support the highway. Plant communities, historical sites, viewsheds, and slopes will also be rated. Each value will be summed at each location and a composite score will be shown. The result is a map showing how suitable each area is for the proposed use. The map shows shades of gray, or a range of colors representing the numeric range of the total scores.

Usually the suitability map shows many irregular shapes and few recognizable patterns. The suitability mapping process works well for site selection, especially when only one or two uses are being sited. However, the suitability map is a poor base for site design because you cannot tell what is happening on the site. You have surrendered your judgment to the numbers. You cannot tell where the tree canopy is, where the marsh is, or where the steep slopes are. The GIS Graphic Method brings the scale of GIS to site levels and shows you what conditions actually exist on the site. Suitability mapping is effective for regional studies, but it is not effective for site design.

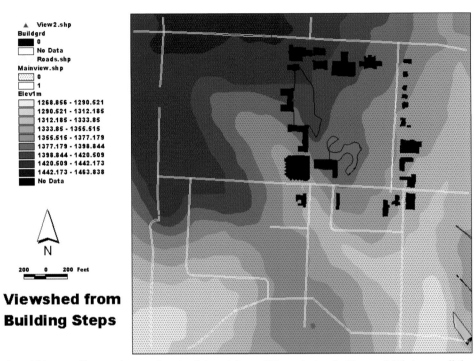

Viewshed from Building Steps

A model is a set of instructions used to simulate certain conditions. A viewshed is a model that maps all the places visible and invisible from a given point. This GIS Graphic Method image shows buildings, roads, and viewsheds over an elevation map.

The landscape architect's site analysis

All the information needed to make design decisions should be clear and understandable when displayed on the site analysis. The site analysis map represents the physical, cadastral, political, and perceptual conditions of the site in a single two-dimensional representation. Both constraints and opportunities, negative and positive conditions, should be shown. Very important criteria might appear more prominently than less important criteria, but legibility is the key to a good site analysis.

The site analysis begins by selecting the critical data while discarding that which is not essential to decision making. Consider these examples of data selection. Slope maps are an important part of any site design, and the categories should reflect functional limits, such as areas that are steep enough to drain, slopes flat enough to meet accessibility requirements, slopes capable of being mowed easily. There are other categories that might apply in certain types of projects, such as a ski resort, that would not be meaningful when designing a city park. Using GIS, the designer selects those slope categories that will be useful and discards those that will not.

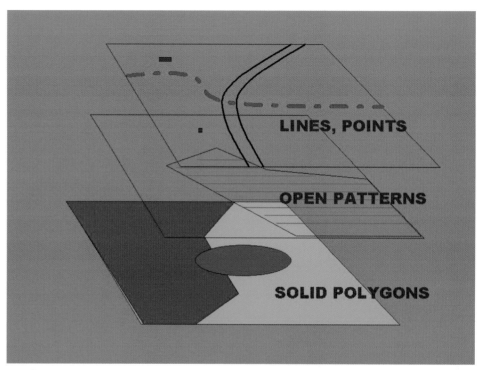

In order to create a site analysis that the designer can understand, the amount of data must be limited and the placement of data in layers must follow the rules shown in this diagram: solid polygons on the bottom, open patterns in the middle, lines and points on top.

What graphic choices are available in the GIS? The Legend Editor allows one to change colors, fill patterns, and line weights with ease. Beyond the graphic choices, the order in which themes are assembled can mean the difference between legibility and confusion. Information can reside in one of three levels: solid polygons on the bottom of the map, open patterned polygons in the middle, and lines, symbols, and labels on top. With ArcView GIS, the development of a site analysis is very simple: as a theme name is moved up or down in the legend, its graphic representation moves up or down in the pile of themes being displayed. This legend hierarchy makes the assembly of the site analysis so simple that anyone, from the landscape architect to the client, can test the themes at different levels.

Once you have decided which types of information are needed for site design, how do you isolate them from the rest? ArcView GIS offers several options.

■ You can use the Query Builder function to select attributes and create a new map of one or more attributes.

■ You can intersect themes, where one theme is used as a cookie cutter to limit the display of another theme. An example of this is selecting all the publicly owned lands from the ownership theme and applying that cookie cutter to vacant lands in the land-use theme. The result shows all the publicly owned vacant land in the study area.

■ The ArcView Spatial Analyst extension can be used to develop meaningful slope, contour, aspect, and hillshade maps from any digital elevation model (DEM).

■ And with the Arcview 3D Analyst extension, you can develop viewshed maps that will become new themes and part of the site analysis.

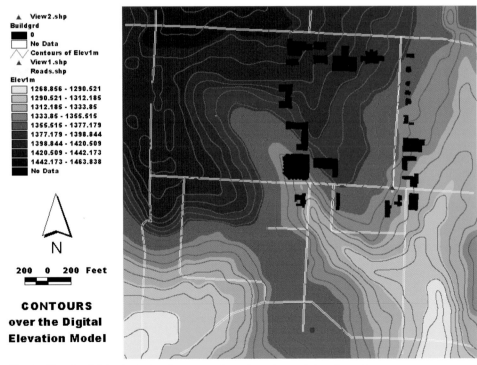

The ArcView Spatial Analyst extension can create contours in any interval you choose.

The next task is to decide on the arrangement of the isolated themes in the site analysis. The least important information resides on the bottom of the site analysis. Where two themes are about equal in importance, one can be on the bottom layer as a solid polygon and the other can be on the middle layer as an open patterned polygon (Hanna and Culpepper, 1998). The patterns selected for the middle layer should have a colored foreground and a transparent background so all the layers can be seen. As a practical matter, two or three solid colored polygons can be displayed on the bottom layer, two or three different open patterns can be shown on the middle layer, and perhaps as many as six line styles and four symbols can be shown on top of the map. Thus, the maximum number of attributes that can be displayed at one time is between twelve and twenty. Again, because each site's characteristics are unique, trial and error is the rule. If the map is too busy, eliminate the least important information.

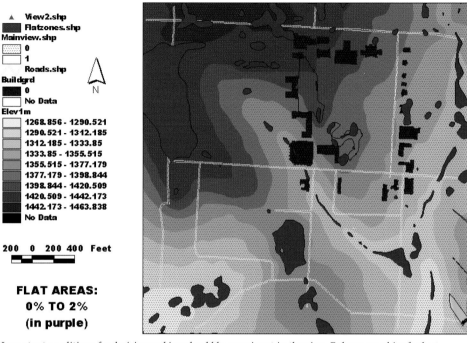

▲ **View2.shp**
■ **Flatzones.shp**
Mainview.shp
▨ 0
☐ 1
Roads.shp
Buildgrd
■ 0
☐ No Data
Elev1m
1268.856 - 1290.521
1290.521 - 1312.185
1312.185 - 1333.85
1333.85 - 1355.515
1355.515 - 1377.179
1377.179 - 1398.844
1398.844 - 1420.509
1420.509 - 1442.173
1442.173 - 1463.838
No Data

N

200 0 200 400 Feet

FLAT AREAS:
0% TO 2%
(in purple)

Important conditions for decision making should be prominent in the view. Balance graphics for best legibility.

At last: Placing the diagrams on the site

Each of the viable spatial diagrams is positioned over the site analysis to create each active zone plan. While several spatial diagrams will adequately represent a particular set of uses and facilities, one or two diagrams will adapt to the site better than the others. It is the mark of a good designer to test several alternatives and to keep testing until the best fit of uses to site has been found.

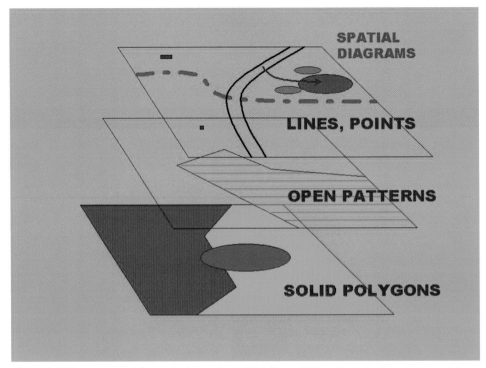

The spatial diagrams are fitted onto the site analysis, following guidelines shown in the program matrices and the layouts shown in the spatial diagrams.

Drawing the use zones and the circulation arrows on the site analysis is done in ArcView GIS with the graphics tools. Several options exist for graphic enhancement. The bubbles and arrows can be drawn in any shape using the free-form polygon tool. The graphics tool has its own legend editor for changing line sizes and styles, and for fill patterns on polygons.

The graphics may be given a degree of transparency so the site analysis can be read beneath the spatial diagram. Once the active zone plan has been generated, the site analysis is no longer needed and an aerial photo can be substituted for the site map. Displayed over an aerial photo, the active zone plan is an image that is easily understood by clients and the public.

Site design is not detail design: site design is small-scale planning. Using GIS for site analysis makes the work of testing alternative active zone plans much more enjoyable.

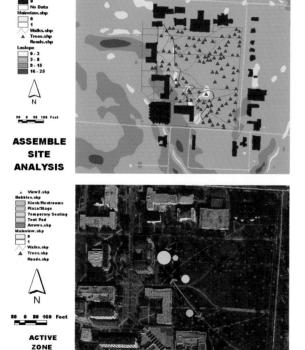

ASSEMBLE SITE ANALYSIS

ACTIVE ZONE PLAN

Over viewshed and aerial photo

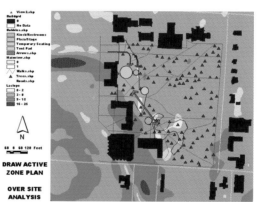

DRAW ACTIVE ZONE PLAN OVER SITE ANALYSIS

In these views, the bottom layer is slope and the middle layer is the viewshed from the red triangle. Trees, sidewalks, buildings, and roads complete the site analysis.

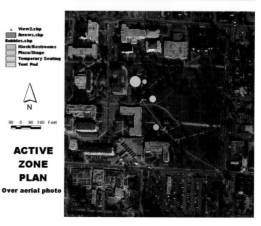

ACTIVE ZONE PLAN

Over aerial photo

Once you have positioned your activity zones, you may replace the site analysis with an aerial photo. Depending on the issues you want to discuss, you may display information over the photo, such as a viewshed or walks, as well as the spatial diagram.

Three-dimensional play

Once the active zone plan has been created, an additional step can make it very
appealing: a three-dimensional view. The
ArcView 3D Analyst extension allows the
designer to display the active zone plan
in three dimensions using a terrain
model as the base. The grid of elevation
points is used to represent the ground
plane. Applying a vertical exaggeration
factor to the elevation points can emphasize the surface variations. The site analysis or an aerial photo can be draped over
this terrain model and rotated to any
viewing angle. The active zone plan is
then displayed in three dimensions over
the site analysis or over the photo. Three-
dimensional views impress widely
diverse audiences.

*Three-dimensional views easily
communicate spatial proposals to
citizens, review boards, clients,
and other professionals.*

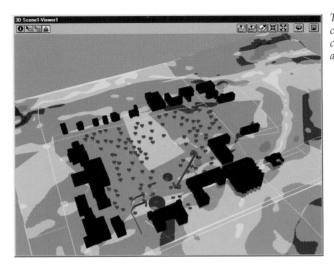

It is a big deal

The advantages of using the GIS Graphic Method are both practical and psychological. Because other design professionals, such as engineers and planners, are using GIS, this method allows landscape architects to serve on design teams with them.

The GIS Graphic Method allows the landscape architect's products to be incorporated directly into the work of other professionals. Civil engineers can use the alignment of an entry drive shown on the active zone plan and imported into CAD to calculate horizontal and vertical alignments. Wildlife specialists can provide GIS model output that the landscape architect can incorporate into the site analysis and subsequent zone plan. The wildlife specialist can then use the active zone plan to quantify the amounts of different types of habitat mitigation and to prepare site-specific management specifications.

Because so many agencies are using GIS, much of their data is available in GIS formats. GIS is becoming the required format for many of these clients, and they expect the sophisticated images and reports that GIS can produce. GIS is becoming the standard for government work and many types of private projects.

Psychologically, the GIS Graphic Method reduces the fear of the unknown. Since the GIS Graphic Method so closely parallels the design process of landscape architects, they can work comfortably, following familiar steps. It is time for landscape architects to join the revolution in design technology.

References

Hanna, Karen C. and R. Brian Culpepper, *GIS in Site Design*, John Wiley & Sons, 1998

McHarg, Ian, *Design with Nature, Second Edition*, McGraw Hill, 1997

Chapter 12

Saving the Salton Sea: A case study in GIS modeling

A GIS MODEL IS A SET OF INSTRUCTIONS for combining spatial elements to yield maps and reports. Models are to GIS users what blueprints are to carpenters, patterns to tailors, and recipes to cooks. The inputs are selected by the user, as are the processes performed on them and the sequence of processing. Soil scientists use GIS models to predict erosion. Police departments use models to schedule patrols. Real estate agents use models to match buyers to available properties. Planners use models to test the potential tax revenues of various zoning proposals. Public works departments use models to estimate annual street repair costs, emergency services to route vehicles, and biologists to estimate wildlife populations. The list of GIS model users is long and varied.

As you have seen in this book, landscape architects use models for comprehensive plans, recreation master planning, visual analyses, site designs, and resource management—models that are as diverse as the designers.

Modeling tools graphically represent the inputs, processes, processing sequences, and outputs of a model. Large or complex models that might be laborious to create without modeling tools are easily created, reused, modified, and shared with them.

ModelBuilder is a set of modeling tools in ArcView Spatial Analyst (a product that extends the spatial analysis capabilities of ArcView GIS). In ModelBuilder, you create a flow diagram that shows the input data, the processing, and the output data for the model. You use icons to represent the data and processes. Lines connecting the icons indicate the sequence of processing. But the flow diagram is not just a graphic; it references real data and GIS processes. It contains all the properties needed to run the spatial processes and create an output map. The data is stored in ArcView GIS. The output map is also stored in ArcView GIS. You can run all or part of the model, and you can adjust the inputs, processes, and outputs as needed.

Many of California's endangered birds, including the bald eagle, seek refuge at the Salton Sea.

Salton Sea: The site of a modeling exercise

The Salton Sea, California's largest inland water body, was accidentally created in December 1904 when a levee broke along the Colorado River. It took two years for engineers to stem the flow of water into the Salton Trough, a desert area more than 200 feet below sea level, and during that time, a huge lake formed. The Salton Sea is currently 35 miles long and 9 to 15 miles wide.

Because other California wetlands are being destroyed, the man-made Salton Sea has become important as a wildlife refuge for fish and birds. More than half the birds using the Pacific Flyway, a bird migration route from Canada to Mexico, now stop at the Salton Sea. It was designated a National Wildlife Refuge in 1925 and has become a home for many endangered species, including desert pupfish, brown pelicans, peregrine falcons, and bald eagles. The Salton Sea is also a fishery and recreational area.

The Salton Sea region

The problem

The Salton Sea is dying. Originally a fresh-water lake, it has become approximately 25 percent more saline than the Pacific Ocean, and the salinity continues to rise. Fresh water does flow into the Salton Sea from agricultural runoff and from streams, but there is no outlet to the Pacific Ocean to remove water and dissolved salts. The water level is maintained through evaporation in the hot desert climate. But as the water evaporates, it leaves behind salts that increase the salinity.

The Salton Sea fishery is predicted to collapse within the next fifteen years if nothing is done to reduce the salinity. Fish and birds are dying in large numbers. Once-thriving resort communities are having trouble attracting tourists because of dead fish and birds, poor water visibility, and odor from large algal blooms.

Working toward a solution

In 1992, Congress created the Salton Sea Authority to restore the sea. The Salton Sea Authority includes local, state, and federal agencies, as well as representatives of the Torres Martinez Desert Cahuilla Indian Tribe, the major landholders in the Salton Sea area. The Salton Sea Authority has been working with the California Department of Water Resources and the Bureau of Reclamation to reduce salinity in the Salton Sea to ocean level. Proposals include constructing dikes and concentration ponds to trap salts, and pumping saline water out to nearby dry lake beds.

The Bureau of Reclamation commissioned the Center for Environmental Management, University of Redlands, to see if GIS technology could be used to help save the Salton Sea. The University of Redlands created the Salton Sea Database Program, a project and Web site (www.cem.uor.edu) that provide scientists and concerned citizens with spatial data and the information they need to decide how best to desalinize the sea.

Building the model

The University of Redlands used ArcView Spatial Analyst and ModelBuilder to explore one proposal to pump saline water from the Salton Sea into nearby dry lake beds. They wanted to show how GIS technology could be used to find the least expensive path for building pipelines.

Using ModelBuilder, they created their model and ran it to generate a map showing the most suitable areas to construct a pipeline.

A simplified version of the model the university team created is shown below. The teal-colored rectangles represent

input data that will be processed by the model. The orange-colored ovals represent the GIS process that will be applied to the data. The brick-colored rounded rectangles represent the output data that will be created by ModelBuilder when the model is run.

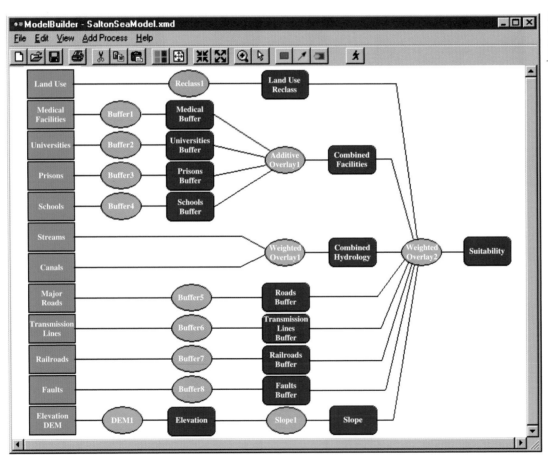

Pipeline construction suitability model for the Salton Sea

Defining the data and the processes

The model included the following data requirements and processes:

Land use

Land use data in the Salton Sea area was reclassified as rural or urban. Farms, ranches, and vacant lands were reclassified as rural, and business and residential districts were reclassified as urban. Rural areas are preferred over urban areas for constructing pipelines because land is cheaper and there are fewer buildings in the way. In the model, the Reclass1 oval represents the reclassification process applied to the land-use data to create the Land Use Reclass data. In the illustration on this page, the Landuse data is the output created by running the Reclass1 process in the model.

Structures to be avoided

Locations of schools, universities, medical facilities, and prisons were mapped. You can see the Schools data to the right. Buffer zones were created around the structures that the model would not allow pipelines to cross. In the model, these buffering processes are represented by the ovals labeled Buffer1, Buffer2, Buffer3, and Buffer4. The output maps from these buffer processes were combined by adding the buffer zones together (the oval labeled Additive Overlay1) to create the Combined Facilities map.

Structures to be favored

Major roads, transmission lines, and railroads are favorable paths for pipeline construction. The right-of-way permits already exist, utilities for construction are likely to be available, and the land is already graded. Buffer zones were also created around these structures, but this time, the model would favor them when finding the most suitable paths. In this model, these buffer processes are represented by the ovals labeled Buffer5, Buffer6, and Buffer7. The results of these buffer processes are the Roads Buffer, Transmission Lines Buffer, and Railroads Buffer map.

Hydrologic considerations

Canals make good paths for pipelines because right-of-way has already been established, but streams should be avoided because they are expensive to cross and easily damaged. In a process called weighted overlay, the canals and streams are given weights according to whether they make good paths, and that data is put together to create the Combined Hydrology map. This process is represented by the oval labeled WeightedOverlay1 in the model.

The input and output data for a model are displayed in ArcView GIS.

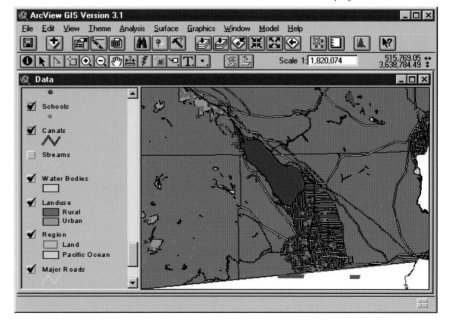

Natural hazards

Two major faults, the San Andreas and the San Jacinto, border the Salton Trough, and many smaller faults criss-cross it. The model creates buffer zones around faults so that these areas will be considered unsuitable for pipelines. The oval labeled Buffer8 represents the buffer process, and the result of the process is the Faults Buffer map.

Slope

The steeper the terrain, the more it costs to build pipelines there. The model converts a digital elevation model (DEM) file, a standard format for elevation data, into grid data, a standard format for ArcView Spatial Analyst, then converts it to a slope map. The oval labeled DEM1 represents the conversion of the DEM file to grid data, and the oval labeled Slope1 represents the conversion of the elevation grid to slope data. The result of the process is the Slope map.

In a final weighted overlay process, the intermediate maps are weighted by how much they contribute to the cost of construction, then the maps are combined. The oval labeled Weighted Overlay2 represents this process. The final result is a Suitability map.

The Suitability map shows the most suitable areas for construction of the desalinization pipelines, given the input data and constraints. When the model is run, it creates the Suitability map in ArcView GIS (shown below). Flat or downhill areas are more suitable and appear in red. Mountainous areas and fault zones representing major obstacles to pipeline construction appear in pink.

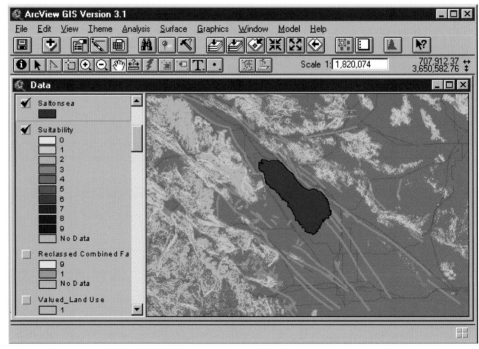

The output map created by ModelBuilder.

Running the model

The University of Redlands team ran the model, then converted the Suitability map into a least-cost path map, which shows the paths with the lowest construction costs. The final map they presented to the Bureau of Reclamation is shown at the right. In the map you can see the paths that are least expensive for pipeline construction. The red areas are the dry lake beds where the salt water could be pumped.

Using ModelBuilder and ArcView GIS, the university team was able to demonstrate how GIS technology could be used to save time and money when investigating alternatives for saving the Salton Sea.

The map showing proposed pipeline paths.

How ModelBuilder performed

The university team designed the pipeline suitability model in four days. It would have taken them weeks to build a model this large without ModelBuilder. The team could come up with ideas to improve the model and test them immediately. They could increase the importance of avoiding streams or decrease the importance of being near transmission lines, and then rerun the model to get new results, all in only a few minutes. ModelBuilder allowed them to spend more time thinking and less time adjusting the model.

The University of Redlands and the Bureau of Reclamation compared the least-cost paths created using GIS tools with those created by hand by engineers working with paper maps. Most of the paths in the two models matched, but a few of the paths differed. The engineers working with paper maps decided that in some areas it would be less expensive to tunnel through steep slopes rather than go around them. The university team could add this constraint into the GIS model and run it again, without redoing all their work.

The University of Redlands team modeled only a part of one proposed solution. This small model can be incorporated into a much larger model as the work progresses. As considerations and constraints become more complex, ModelBuilder's importance will grow.

What GIS modeling tools can and cannot do

A modeling tool like ModelBuilder allows landscape architects to concentrate on their specialty instead of spending a lot of time learning how to run GIS software. GIS models can be shared with other professionals on the design team, reviewing agencies, design review committees, lending institutions, and community groups. Because the model is graphical, it is easier to explain it to clients. Because it is so effortless to refine your model, it is likely that you will examine several alternatives. You can also publish standard models on the Web to share them with your entire industry.

What a GIS modeling tool cannot do is replace the expertise, good judgement, and ethical standards of the professionals using these tools. These tools cannot improve poor-quality data or identify flawed logic and inaccurate assumptions. Therein lies the danger. Because they are easy to use, GIS modeling tools can also be misused, but the resulting maps look so professional that it may be difficult to spot problems.

As GIS modeling tools become more powerful, they will become even more popular with planners and site designers. The graphical modeling methods in tools like ModelBuilder will enable landscape architects to join their design colleagues as GIS users.

Conclusion

GIS does not replace the need for tracing paper and soft pencils, but it provides better basemaps for designing. GIS is inclusive, efficient, and flexible. It is the state of the art.

GIS is inclusive because it allows all the design team members, as well as ad hoc committees, outside experts, and reviewing agencies, to work at the same scale and resolution. It allows the results of any exercise to be shared in a common, digital format. Everyone on a design team is looking at the same symbols, the same scale, and the same attributes.

GIS is efficient because it allows vast quantities of data to be analyzed in a short time, with reduced production costs. With a GIS, it is quite simple to run several variations on a single model, or on entirely different sets of models. Since the GIS allows inexpensive trials, more time can be spent researching methods and devising new models, rather than on the execution of each model.

GIS is efficient because all the files are conveniently stored and accessed through the computer. All the operations take place inside the computer without rolls of tracing paper, or Mylar® overlays cluttering up the office, waiting to be filed.

The graphic abilities of GIS have improved dramatically in recent years, in part due to the simplicity of graphical user interfaces. Graphic representations have also improved to include much of the richness of hand-drawn symbols with variable line weights, fill patterns, and fonts. GIS allows the maps produced by all the members on the team to look alike. GIS maps can be imported into other programs for easy, professional production of plans and reports.

One of the dangers in GIS is that poor judgments can be difficult to identify among the vast number of operations. When a designer's logic is not sound, certain bad judgments can reinforce one another. The Delphi Method is one way of avoiding flaws in the judgment of a single person. Because a group of people is making decisions, errors in judgment are less likely. Round after round of Delphi input, community polling, or other consensus-building methods are easy to incorporate in a GIS.

As generalists, landscape architects are ideal leaders for design teams. However, leaders must understand the technology if they are to lead decisively. GIS expands the opportunities for interaction on the team, giving landscape architects meaningful dialog earlier in the project. Because the operations are recorded, especially with ModelBuilder, there is less mystique;

every operation is documented and shared with others on the team. Your decisions can be questioned by others, as can theirs.

Many clients are beginning to insist on GIS formats, even when the project does not justify it. As more and more spatial data is generated in GIS format, the non-digital maps fail to be updated, so manual methods are increasingly difficult to use. The CAD–GIS interface is becoming seamless, allowing clients to continue using CAD along with GIS. In the very near future, geographic data will be available only in digital form.

Just as landscape architects must know how to read road profiles to work effectively with civil engineers, they must also know how to take advantage of the information available in the files of cities and counties. Cities, water districts, and utility providers have long been important clients for landscape architects. As these clients continue to participate in digital data gathering, they make GIS one of their important operating tools. So must we.

Books from **ESRI Press**

The ESRI Guide to GIS Analysis, Volume 1: Geographic Patterns and Relationships
An important book about how to do real analysis with a geographic information system. *The ESRI Guide to GIS Analysis* focuses on six of the most common geographic analysis tasks. ISBN 1-879102-06-4 188 pages

Modeling Our World: The ESRI Guide to Geodatabase Design
With this comprehensive guide and reference to GIS data modeling and to the new geodatabase model introduced with ArcInfo™ 8, you will learn how to make the right decisions about modeling data, from database design and data capture to spatial analysis and visual presentation. ISBN 1-879102-62-5 216 pages

Hydrologic and Hydraulic Modeling Support with Geographic Information Systems
This book presents the invited papers in water resources at the 1999 ESRI® International User Conference. Covering practical issues related to hydrologic and hydraulic water quantity modeling support using GIS, the concepts and techniques apply to any hydrologic and hydraulic model requiring spatial data or spatial visualization. ISBN 1-879102-80-3 232 pages

Beyond Maps: GIS and Decision Making in Local Government
Beyond Maps shows how local governments are making geographic information systems true management tools. Packed with real-life examples, it explores innovative ways to use GIS to improve local government operations. ISBN 1-879102-79-X 240 pages

The ESRI Press Dictionary of GIS Terminology
This long-needed and authoritative reference brings together the language and nomenclature of the many GIS-related disciplines and applications. Designed for students, professionals, researchers, and technicians, the dictionary provides succinct and accurate definitions of more than a thousand terms. ISBN 1-879102-78-1 128 pages

Planning Support Systems: Integrating Geographic Information Systems, Models, and Visualization Tools
Richard Brail of Rutgers University's Edward J. Bloustein School of Planning and Public Policy, and Richard Klosterman of the University of Akron, have assembled papers from colleagues around the globe who are working to expand the applicability and understanding of the top issues in computer-aided planning. ISBN 1-58948-011-2 468 pages

Geographic Information Systems and Science
This comprehensive guide to GIS, geographic information science (GIScience), and GIS management illuminates some shared concerns of business, government, and science. It looks at how issues of management, ethics, risk, and technology intersect, and at how GIS provides a gateway to problem solving, and links to special learning modules at ESRI Virtual Campus (campus.esri.com). ISBN 0-471-89275-0 472 pages

Undersea with GIS
Explore how GIS is illuminating the mysteries hidden in the earth's oceans. Applications include managing protected underwater sanctuaries, tracking whale migration, and recent advances in 3-D electronic navigation. The companion CD brings the underwater world to life for both the undersea practitioner and student and includes 3-D underwater fly-throughs, ArcView® extensions for marine applications, a K–12 lesson plan, and more. ISBN 1-58948-016-3 276 pages

Past Time, Past Place: GIS for History
In this pioneering book that encompasses the Greek and Roman eras, the Salem witch trials, the Dust Bowl of the 1930s, and much more, leading scholars explain how GIS technology can illuminate the study of history. Richly illustrated, *Past Time, Past Place* is a vivid supplement to many courses in cultural studies and will fascinate armchair historians. ISBN 1-58948-032-5 224 pages

Arc Hydro: GIS for Water Resources
Based on ESRI ArcGIS® software, the Arc Hydro data model provides a new and standardized way of describing hydrologic data to consistently and efficiently solve water resource problems at any spatial scale. This book is a blueprint of the model and the definitive overview of GIS in hydrology from the field's leading expert. The companion CD includes Arc Hydro instructions, tools, teacher resources, and data. ISBN 1-58948-034-1 220 pages

Confronting Catastrophe: A GIS Handbook
This hands-on manual is for GIS practitioners and decision makers whose communities face the threat of large-scale disasters, whether they be wildfires, hurricanes, earthquakes, or now, terrorist attacks. Real-world lessons show public officials and IT managers how to use GIS most efficiently in the five stages of disaster management: identification and planning, mitigation, preparedness, response, and recovery. ISBN 1-58948-040-6 156 pages

A System for Survival: GIS and Sustainable Development
The goal of sustainable development is to raise standards of living worldwide without depleting resources or destroying habitat. This book shows how geographic technologies, by synthesizing the vast amounts of data being collected about natural resources, population, health, public safety, and more, can play a creative and constructive role in realizing that goal. ISBN 1-58948-052-X 124 pages

Marine Geography: GIS for the Oceans and Seas
This collection of case studies documents some of the many current applications of marine GIS. The contributing authors share their work, challenges, successes, and progress in the use of GIS, and show how the technology is being used to influence the decision-making process in a way that leads to healthy and sustainable oceans and seas. ISBN 1-58948-045-7 224 pages

Thinking About GIS: Geographic Information System Planning for Managers
Dr. Roger Tomlinson, the "father of GIS," distills in these pages the wisdom gleaned from a career spent launching successful GIS implementations worldwide. The author's proven and practical method for implementing a GIS will benefit senior GIS and IT managers and technical managers and give both groups a common platform on which to conduct serious GIS planning. ISBN 1-58948-070-8 304 pages

Advanced Spatial Analysis: The CASA Book of GIS
This book describes cutting-edge developments in GIS applications at University College London's Centre for Advanced Spatial Analysis. Drawn from archaeology, architecture, cartography, computer science, geography, planning, remote sensing, geomatic engineering, and transport studies, these applications are emerging as the basis for wide-ranging spatial decision-support systems. ISBN 1-58948-073-2 472 pages

Connecting Our World: GIS Web Services
As the Internet and World Wide Web revolutionize GIS and spatial data use in fundamental ways, GIS Web services are a natural progression in the development of the technology. A dozen of the most innovative GIS Web services drawn from around the world are highlighted in this essential guide, a must-read for forward-looking managers in any enterprise. ISBN 1-58948-075-9 178 pages

CONTINUED ON NEXT PAGE

The Case Studies Series

ArcView GIS Means Business

Written for business professionals, this book is a behind-the-scenes look at how some of America's most successful companies have used desktop GIS technology. The book is loaded with full-color illustrations and comes with a trial copy of ArcView software and a GIS tutorial. ISBN 1-879102-51-X 136 pages

Zeroing In: Geographic Information Systems at Work in the Community

In twelve "tales from the digital map age," this book shows how people use GIS in their daily jobs. An accessible and engaging introduction to GIS for anyone who deals with geographic information. ISBN 1-879102-50-1 128 pages

Managing Natural Resources with GIS

Find out how GIS technology helps people design solutions to such pressing challenges as wildfires, urban blight, air and water degradation, species endangerment, disaster mitigation, coastline erosion, and public education. The experiences of public and private organizations provide real-world examples. ISBN 1-879102-53-6 132 pages

Enterprise GIS for Energy Companies

A volume of case studies showing how electric and gas utilities use geographic information systems to manage their facilities more cost effectively, find new market opportunities, and better serve their customers. ISBN 1-879102-48-X 120 pages

Transportation GIS

From monitoring rail systems and airplane noise levels, to making bus routes more efficient and improving roads, the twelve case studies in this book show how geographic information systems have emerged as the tool of choice for transportation planners. ISBN 1-879102-47-1 132 pages

GIS for Landscape Architects

From Karen Hanna, noted landscape architect and GIS pioneer, comes *GIS for Landscape Architects*. Through actual examples, you will learn how landscape architects, land planners, and designers now rely on GIS to create visual frameworks within which spatial data and information are gathered, interpreted, manipulated, and shared. ISBN 1-879102-64-1 120 pages

GIS for Health Organizations

Health management is a rapidly developing field, where even slight shifts in policy affect the health care we receive. In this book, you will see how physicians, public health officials, insurance providers, hospitals, epidemiologists, researchers, and HMO executives use GIS to focus resources to meet the needs of those in their care. ISBN 1-879102-65-X 112 pages

GIS in Public Policy: Using Geographic Information for More Effective Government

This book shows how policy makers and others on the front lines of public service are putting GIS to work—to carry out the will of voters and legislators, and to inform and influence their decisions. *GIS in Public Policy* shows vividly the very real benefits of this new digital tool for anyone with an interest in, or influence over, the ways our institutions shape our lives. ISBN 1-879102-66-8 120 pages

Integrating GIS and the Global Positioning System

The Global Positioning System is an explosively growing technology. *Integrating GIS and the Global Positioning System* covers the basics of GPS and presents several case studies that illustrate some of the ways the power of GPS is being harnessed to GIS, ensuring, among other benefits, increased accuracy in measurement and completeness of coverage. ISBN 1-879102-81-1 112 pages

GIS in Schools

GIS is transforming classrooms—and learning—in elementary, middle, and high schools across North America. *GIS in Schools* documents what happens when students are exposed to GIS. The book gives teachers practical ideas about how to implement GIS in the classroom, and some theory behind the success stories. ISBN 1-879102-85-4 128 pages

Disaster Response: GIS for Public Safety

GIS is improving emergency management response to natural disasters, providing a comprehensive and effective system of preparedness, mitigation, response, and recovery. Case studies describe GIS use in siting fire stations, routing emergency response vehicles, controlling wildfires, assisting earthquake victims, improving public disaster preparedness, and much more. ISBN 1-879102-88-9 124 pages

Open Access: GIS in e-Government

A revolution taking place on the Web is transforming the traditional relationship between government and citizens. At the forefront of this e-government revolution are agencies using GIS to serve interactive maps over their Web sites and, in the process, empower citizens. This book presents case studies of a cross section of these forward-thinking agencies. ISBN 1-879102-87-0 124 pages

GIS in Telecommunications

Global competition is forcing telecommunications companies to stretch their boundaries as never before—requiring efficiency and innovation in every aspect of the enterprise if they are to survive, prosper, and come out on top. The ten case studies in this book detail how telecommunications competitors worldwide are turning to GIS to give them the edge they need. ISBN 1-879102-86-2 120 pages

Conservation Geography: Case Studies in GIS, Computer Mapping, and Activism

GIS is revolutionizing the work of nonprofit organizations and conservation groups worldwide as they rush to save the earth's plants, animals, and cultural and natural resources. This collection of dozens of case studies shows how computers and GIS are transforming the way environmental problems and conservation issues are identified, measured, and ultimately, resolved. ISBN 1-58948-024-4 252 pages

GIS Means Business, Volume Two

Both business professionals and general readers will find in these pages many new examples of companies and organizations—a chamber of commerce, a credit union, colleges, reinsurance and real estate firms, and more—that have used ESRI software to solve problems, make smarter decisions, enhance customer service, and discover new markets and profit opportunities. ISBN 1-58948-033-3 188 pages

Mapping the News: Case Studies in GIS and Journalism

Ten case studies show newsroom managers, journalists, and student journalists how GIS and computer-assisted reporting are revolutionizing the news business. Packed with full-color illustrations, maps, and other graphics, this important guide also contains an introduction to GIS. Two detailed appendixes help journalists start fast with GIS and learn how to acquire free data. ISBN 1-58948-072-4 168 pages